BEING & RACE

BEING

& RACE *Black Writing since 1970*

CHARLES JOHNSON

*Indiana
University* BLOOMINGTON AND INDIANAPOLIS
Press

First Midland Book Edition 1990

© 1988 by Charles Johnson

Manufactured in the United States of America

Library of Congress Cataloging-in-Publication Data
Johnson, Charles Richard, 1948–
  Being and race.
  Includes index.
    1. American literature—Afro-American authors—
History and criticism.   2. American literature—
20th century—History and criticism.   3. Afro-Americans
in literature.   4. Phenomenology and literature.
I. Title.
PS153.N5J63   1987   810′.9′896073   86-46405
ISBN 0-253-31165-9
ISBN 0-253-20537-9 (pbk.)

3 4 5 6 7 94 93 92 91 90

For Malik and Elizabeth

In fiction there must be a theoretical basis to the most minute details. Even a single glove must have its theory.
—Prosper Mérimée

■ Contents

Preface

At times, and when I felt it necessary, this book makes use of the method called "phenomenology," a term often misunderstood, like so many in popular use. Many different styles of phenomenology have been developed since mathematician Edmund Husserl, its creator, proposed it as a means for grounding the principal concepts in any field by a return to "experience." Husserl's own "Transcendental Phenomenology" was judged too idealistic by some of his followers, who took, as I have, what they found useful from the master and went their own way. Max Scheler, who was at one time Husserl's heir apparent, devoted a portion of his phenomenological work to investigating the experiential foundations for morality and religion. Martin Heidegger, Husserl's real successor in my view, eventually broke with phenomenology, preferring to call his work not even philosophy but instead "thought on Being." Jean-Paul Sartre, whose existentialist commitments often overlap Heidegger's, infused his tremendous literary outpourings with social theory, such as Marxism, that situated the transcendental ego and this mode of reasoning more firmly in the realm of immediate political and historical phenomena than in the transcendent realm of pure meaning that occupied Husserl. It is Sartre's associate Maurice Merleau-Ponty, however, who most significantly advances Husserlian thought by developing his central notion of the Lifeworld, and he is distinguished by his own work on dialectical theory, language, perception, and the body as our foundation for all perceptual experience and by avoiding many of the excesses and errors of Sartre's philosophy. Equally important is Mikel Dufrenne, whose blending of Husserl, Heidegger, Sartre, Merleau-Ponty, and Roman Ingarten focuses some of the more interesting work of the German and French phenomenological movements on the problems of artistic experience broadly considered.

It will be clear from this book that my own quirky variations on phenomenology draw from the work of these esteemed gentlemen, as well as from that of many other philosophers, Eastern and Western. Nevertheless, throughout its long history, and despite its many changes, phenomenology remains a "philosophy of experience." Husserl's intention was for it to be first a method by which we "bracket," or set aside, all explanatory models for the phenomena we investigate, thereby making possible an intuition of the essence or invariant structures of different forms of experience, specifically in the sciences. His famous call, "To the things themselves," distinguishes phenomenology from previous disciplines of philosophy. Phenomenology is something you *do*. Yet it does not so much deliver new knowledge as it does a deeper clarification of what we think we already know. And what truth its method delivers must be confirmed in the depths of the reader's own experience. It is, for Husserl, a "radical empiricism." Whether or not we believe it is possible to disclose the atemporal essences of things, as Husserl hoped, is unimportant. His method of bracketing and descriptively reporting what is given in any encounter with mathematical, fantastical, physical, or fictional objects is useful for a first-person determination of what is before us, and for revealing what we, as culturally conditioned subjects, have brought to each and every encounter with the world. Moreover, it is a method more commonly used than most realize. Painters, as Merleau-Ponty tirelessly pointed out, must retrain their eyes in seeing; musicians, their ears in hearing; and writers, in the being of language. And many art critics instinctively perform various phenomenological operations—free imaginative variation or consideration of the all-important element of intentionality—in order better to grasp their subject and to ground it in their own first-person seeing before moving on to judgment, analysis, condemnation, or approval.

But it is Husserl's other, more programmatic aim that has forced this work on black writing to fall into a phenomenological mode: namely, his belief that many disciplines and fields of knowing rest on unclarified, naive assumptions that need to be brought forward if these fields are to achieve a securer foundation. Black American fiction, indeed the entire area of "creative writing," has not seen its basic assumptions subjected to this form of discussion. I believe the time for that is now. My deepest hope is that this book will contribute to the dialogue, especially now, when cross-cultural meaning is of such great importance. And it is also my hope that it will be useful not only to teachers and students of Afro-American literature but also to those in philosophy, creative writing, and contemporary literature.

In this task I am indebted to former teachers such as visual artist Lawrence Lariar, who taught me drawing in my teens, and the late John Gardner, who taught me fiction in my twenties; to John Gallman, whose sustained interest made this book possible; to agents Anne and Georges Borchardt; to many friends, among them bookseller Jeff Rice, poet James Bertolino, director Jon Dichter; and to my colleagues at the University of Washington and the University of Delaware, who provided a climate suitable for the book's composition.

First Philosophy

1

■ *Being and Race*

■ A novelist blundering into the field of literary criticism should first apologize to his colleagues who analyze fiction for a living and then make some effort to explain why he has briefly left the business of writing stories to talk about them. My credentials for this chore are modest, but my curiosity about how fiction "works" is great. It has been so from the first day I took up writing. Life is baffling enough for every novelist, and for writers of Afro-American fiction it presents even more artistic and philosophical questions than for writers who are white. Few writers, black or white, bother with such questions, and in the long run they may have importance only to a few people who wonder, as I have for twenty years, about the forms our stories have taken, what they say about the world, and what they don't say. These are not idle questions. Our faith in fiction comes from an ancient belief that language and literary art—all speaking and showing—clarify our experience. Our most sacred cliché in contemporary criticism, and also in creative-writing courses, is that writers should "write about what they know," and for the Afro-American author that inevitably means the "black" experience. This idea is doubtlessly true, or at least half-true in some narrow sense we have yet to determine. But it leads, I believe, from loose, casual talk about "experience" to esthetic and epistemological questions difficult to answer, though I shall try in this book to do so.

It might be helpful to digress a moment to dwell on the artistic impulse itself. Do we *begin* at the same place, writers black and white? In his study of painting, *The Voices of Silence*, André Malraux says, "What makes the artist is that in his youth he was more deeply moved by his visual experience of works of art than by that of the things they represent—and perhaps of Nature as a whole."[1] He adds, "We have no means of knowing how a great artist, who had never seen a work of art, but only the forms of nature, would develop." In other words, we *encounter* art in some form, blunder onto it—or have it placed before us by teachers or parents—as a being different from others in the world. Many black authors confess in interviews that the origin of their artistic journey began when, as children, they heard folktales or ghost stories in the South from elders; and one young American novelist, whom I won't name, is known to say he decided to write when, after passing an auditorium where a distinguished author was reading, he thought to himself, "I can do *that.*" It helps, clearly, if a novice writer has a healthy sense of contempt for his predecessors, or if one's first exposure is, let us say, to easy art rather than to something as intimidating as *Hamlet* or Thomas Mann's *Doktor Faustus.* My own students and friends, once polled, reported an array of first impressions or seductions—Nancy Drew novels, picture books of Bible stories, "Twilight Zone" episodes, Marvel comic books, science fiction, "The Little Engine That Could," or stories they were assigned to read from *Scholastic* magazine. For American kids, it seems to matter little whether they cut their teeth on Louis L'Amour's westerns or Aesop's fables before moving on to more complex novels. Novelist John Gardner often cited his primary influences as Walt Disney and Jean-Paul Sartre, and his best-known book, *Grendel,* seems to bear this out. It's important to remember that this early seduction of the artist by some artwork, vulgar or distinguished, is experienced as delightful—thrilling *as* a story or novel or poem, an encounter that pleases one that such a thing as this can be. Now, delight need not be joyful. I daresay we take pleasure in encounters that shake us to the core, terrorize us, or contradict our most cherished beliefs as well as in those that leave us feeling smug. But in many of these earliest encounters we discover we have been changed. More precisely, our perception—or way of seeing—has been shaken, if one is talking about great art, which is all I care to consider here. In a word, writers begin their lifelong odyssey in art with expression or experience *interpreted* by others, not with, as popular wisdom sometimes has it, an ensemble of events that already mean something.

Going even further, Malraux tells us that "artists do not stem from their childhood, but from their conflicts with the achievements of their predecessors; not from their formless world, but from their struggle with the forms which others have imposed on life." Some of this curious idea can be seen in, for example, figure-drawing classes, where you stand with the canvas to your side and with brush poised as you study the model at the front of the room, and then, miraculously, something happens in the flickerish moment between shifting your gaze from the model, with all his concrete, specific, individual features, to the canvas. You have drawn, you discover, not *his* hand but instead your *idea* of how a hand should look, an idea built up doubtlessly from viewing, not hundreds of individual models, but rather other artists' renditions of the hand. It is precisely this heavily conditioned seeing, this calcification of perception, that figure-drawing classes seek to liberate—we might well call this retraining of the eye the artist's equivalent to the phenomeno-logical *epoché,* or "bracketing" of all presuppositions in order to seize a fresh, original vision.

Malraux's point is that often the apprentice artist, thinking about the world of experience transfigured in the text—a novel, painting, poem, or film—says, "That's not so." Or, "He didn't get it quite right." He might also say, "How perfectly done. Let *me* reply with a composition of my own." Whatever the case, fiction—indeed, all art—points to others with whom the writer argues about what *is.* He cannot begin *ex nihilo.* He must have models with which to agree, partly agree, or outright oppose, and these can come only from the tradition of literature itself, for Nature seems to remain silent, providing no final text or court of judgment. If any of these ruminations sound reasonable, does it seem possible that the "black experience" in literature truly exists only there—*in* litera-ture—and therefore must vary from one author's viewpoint to the next, with nothing invariant in the "experience" that we can agree on as final?

As a young novelist, I found the problem of what is or is not the "black" experience staring at me more steadily than I could stare at it, particularly after I'd written six bad, apprentice novels, three that aped the style of James Baldwin, Richard Wright, and John A. Williams, all fine writers whom I admire, and three that were heavily influenced by what a few critics now call the "Black Aesthetic." The first three of the six were misery-filled protest stories about the sorry condition of being black in America and might be called "naturalistic." I couldn't read them after they were done. Something was wrong, but I couldn't jump the problem until years later when I realized how uncritical I'd been about nearly every aspect of fiction, each element in this discipline being somewhat like a thread, which, if pulled, leads on to the unraveling of an entire garment. Surely naturalism in its various strains is suitable for certain kinds of stories, and for a certain social message, but lost in it for a time I ran into artistic restrictions I couldn't resolve, never realizing that writ-ing doesn't so much record an experience— or even imitate or represent it—as it *creates* that experience, and that each literary form, style, or genre is a different, distinct method of reasoning, of shaping what is to body it forth intelligibly.

In hindsight, naturalism seemed to conceal profound prejudices about Being, what a person is, the nature of society, causation, and a worm can of metaphysical questions about what could and could not logically occur in our "experience" and conscious life. Its implied physics was dated—or at best only provisional—and, even worse, it concealed a reductionistic model of human psychology, of what motivates men and women (and had no theory of the self at all), that made my characters dull and predictable in their inner lives and perceptions of the world. Like gravity, it held the imagination close to the ground by creating the camera-like illusion of objectivity, of events unmediated— or untampered with—by any narrative presence. Although easy to imitate as a style, it scaled down experiential possibilities and put curious limits on narrative voice and language, as well as on such poetic devices as simile and metaphor, those inherently existential strategies that allow a writer to pluck similarities from our experiences or to illuminate one object by reference to another by saying A *is* B. We shall soon look more closely at whether metaphor is mere illusion, a mind trick or trap that dangerously anthropomorphizes the world. For now it is enough simply to say that naturalism gained its power, its punch, by strictly controlling what could be said, seen, and shown.

Adopting such means uncritically, I discovered by error what novelist Linsey Abrams seemed to know by instinct, that "style is never simply technical choice, but evolves from how a writer sees the world." In her brilliant essay "A Maximalist Novelist Looks at Some Minimalist Fiction" (1985), she says that to embrace a "readily identifiable prose style without being aware of its tyranny and inevitability of voice" is to embrace "a ready-made point-of-view." In short, naturalism is clearly a massaging and kneading of life, a style as full of tricks and false bottoms as any other. Of course, none of these observations is new. Philosopher Edmund Husserl (and also Albert Schweitzer) said as much seventy years ago in his criticism of the "Natural Attitude." And so, like the editors who read those three early efforts of mine, I had no interest in revisiting their fictional worlds ever again.

Not much later I foundered again, this time with three novels created under the spell of the Black Arts Movement, the "cultural wing" of the Black Power Movement, which was inescapable in the late 1960s and which is more or less alive today as a quasi-philosophical position with its roots deep in Pan-Africanism and race pride. In order to understand black fiction, its problems and promise, and why these last novels I've mentioned were artistic failures, you must appreciate some of the pitfalls to be found in the history of black American literature and what confronts a young writer when he considers his place in this still relatively young tradition.

The political and social status of the work of art has been a point of interest since the earliest philosophical reflections on poetry. "It is phantoms, not realities that they produce," Plato's Socrates says of the artist in the tenth book of *The Republic.*[2] If a preestablished model is assumed for our experience, or for *any* experience—if meaning is seen as fixed rather than as evolving, changing, and historical, if reality is reified for political or social or even moral reasons—the independent writer who departs from the "forms" can only be seen as one who "sets up in each individual soul a vicious constitution by fashioning phantoms far removed from reality," or what is taken to be the "objective" model for the Real. And so Socrates banishes all but a few poets from the republic, retaining only those who write hymns and praises. Although twenty-five centuries separate us from *The Republic,* the problems raised by black fiction return us to Plato's musings, for nowhere are the questions of social and political relevance in literature more pronounced than in this body of American literature.

From its beginnings in the poetry of Phillis Wheatley and the narrative of Gustavus Vassa, black fiction comprises, one must confess, an overwhelmingly tragic literature. It is full of failures. A catalogue of man's inhumanity to man and woman. Book after book discloses the desperate struggle of a people first to survive against stupendous odds and then to secure the most basic rights in a perpetually hostile environment. Whites in this history act; blacks can only *re*act.

The black American novel begins with *Clotelle, or the Colored Heroine* (1853) by William Wells Brown. *Clotelle* has always been regarded as a pivotal book in black letters insofar as many critics have used it as a departure point for two directions in nineteenth century black writing—the tradition of black social criticism and the novel. Always, and forever, these forms must be understood in terms of the catastrophe of American slavery, detailed fully by Frederick Douglass and others in slave narratives that are the ancestral roots of black fiction. It is a bloody history of atrocity, of stripping a people of cultural identity, then grotesquely caricaturing them in the national (white) imagination. The burden on the free, literate black population was staggering—to lead the antislavery effort, counteract the ideology of racism, and prove themselves worthy of equality. Two tendencies—a clear dialectic—surely exist here at the beginning of black fiction, as critic Addison Gayle, Jr., argues in his study *The Way of the New World* (1975). In the writings of Martin Delany, a man of many literary and political accomplishments, and in those of Sutton Griggs, we find the first glimmerings of black separatism in their call for blacks to consider migrating to other lands to escape oppression (an idea also entertained by Abraham Lincoln), while Douglass, W. E. B. Du Bois, and others developed writings that were integrationist—indeed, for Du Bois (who probably studied Hegel during his days at Harvard), integration was not simply a way of social organization but the dialectical process of evolution itself, a movement that as it pushed society forward would preserve the essential elements in such polarities as black and white. Historically, the black novel appears close to the hour that post–Civil War gains in the South toppled, as Reconstruction's advances were rolled back—one of the most violent periods of black history when, between 1885 and 1900, 2,500 blacks were lynched: an average of about one murder every third day. This was the time of Douglass's death; of Booker T. Washington's ascension; and of repression: white southern reaction in the form of Jim Crow legislation, "black codes," and revivified racial stereotypes.

Here we can only sketch that history, but it is, on the whole and in general, a nightmare. The black American writer begins his or her career with—and continues to exhibit—a crisis of identity. If anything, black fiction is *about* the troubled quest for identity and liberty, the agony of social alienation, the longing for a real and at times a mythical home. Something similar, of course, can be said of early American writers in respect to their struggle to break with European culture and to carve out an "American" sense of selfhood. In his literary manifesto, "Blueprint for Negro Writing" (1937), Richard Wright suggests that eighteenth- and nineteenth-century black writers composed fiction and poetry to impress whites with their humanity and thereby to win for themselves a more comfortable place in the racial world. If Wright is even half-correct about this, then we must say, tentatively, that a serious question for early black fiction was audience. For whom did one write? In the language of the time—neoclassical verse larded with sentiment if one were a Wheatley—and not in black folk idioms, at least not until

Paul Lawrence Dunbar produced dialect verse about plantation life
(humorously portrayed) that tragically became both a showcase and a
trap for his poetic talents. His white sponsors and audience would
accept nothing else, though some of Dunbar's standard-English poems
are outstanding. But this was not the only artistic problem that faced
early black authors.

In *The Negro Novel in America* (1958), critic Robert Bone points out
a more serious problem, the necessity of developing well-rounded
black characters (and I would add white ones as well) to balance the
degrading stereotypes created by whites in the post-Reconstruction
period, a problem that still shadows all black fiction today and one to
which we shall return. The black novel, Bone says, began at the tail end
of the romantic tradition, opting for the then fading strategy of melodrama, but still retained a strong abolitionist flavor from its origins in
the slave narrative. According to Bone, melodrama deals primarily with
issues of Right and Wrong. His evaluation of early black novels bears
much truth, but we should not blink away the beauty, the charm, and the
artistic interest to be found in such pivotal writers as Charles Chesnutt,
who achieved in imaginative short stories such as "The Goophered
Grapevine" and "The Passing of Grandison" levels of irony, ingenuity,
and invention that are, even by today's standards, pretty satisfying. More,
Chesnutt's work reveals a great deal about the genesis of the modern
American short story, for it is during his time that writers were wrestling
with definitions of this form, trying to distinguish it from the tale and the
novella. His tales published in *The Conjure Woman* (1899) are just
that—tales that recall the work of Washington Irving and Nathaniel
Hawthorne. Yet they are structurally informed by the story form of the
late 1800s. It is Edgar Allan Poe who first clarified the form in his crucial
essay, "The Philosophy of Composition" (1842); here he gives primacy
to brevity and emotional effect in the short story. Those elements are
later formularized by O. Henry in such stories as "The Gift of the Magi"
and held up as models for effective storytelling in writing handbooks
published around the turn of the century: the brisk, tightly plotted
magazine story that emphasizes a twist or reversal and that contains a
touch of fantasy (Rod Serling's better "Twilight Zone" tales are a mod-
ern-day descendant of this nineteenth-century form). And does this kind
of story have drawbacks? Yes, if you place great value on character in
fiction, for this form generally only permits types, people given only the
slightest brush strokes for development so that the forward motion of

events can proceed steadily and unhampered to a denouement. For all these faults, Chesnutt manages in such stories as "The Wife of His Youth" the at times remarkable feat of transforming elements of the slave experience into light yet serious entertainment and never minimalizes the pathos of bondage. They are stories rich in humor, which always means that a writer has distance from his material, and equally rich in suspense, a charming Jamesian narrative voice, and gentle but effective social criticism. In these tales, love of unusual characters and life's surprises replace the grind and grim predictability of melodrama, which as a strategy does not so much probe values as it exhorts, indicts, accuses. Bone argues, and rightly I think, that but for one or two exceptions the universe of early black fiction did little to expand beyond this less than complex treatment of racial affairs.

The Harlem Renaissance, which spanned the 1920s, has been much discussed, most interestingly by historian Nathan Huggins. It is usually explained in terms of large-scale developments in black history such as the black migrations from southern repression to the northern factory cities; the development of Harlem as a black cultural center in the East; the rise of a black middle class, heir to the social ethic of Booker T. Washington and his program for self-help; and the cultural impact when West Indians, Africans, and American blacks found themselves side-by-side in Harlem. Also, it was the time of Marcus Garvey's United Negro Improvement Association (predecessor first to the Nation of Islam, then to Louis Farrakhan), a back-to-Africa movement inspired by Washington's separatist philosophy and led by a theatrical little man who envisioned universal black liberation and the shoring up of Africa as a modern nation-state styled on the culture of England, complete with black kings and queens and the Black Star Shipping Line. For whites, it was the period when the Negro became . . . well, "interesting." But for all the wrong reasons. In the period of national exhaustion following World War I, a somewhat weary America grew interested in Sigmund Freud's idea that civilization is based on the repression of eros and became suspicious of tight-sphinctered Victorian values, which many Negroes shared nevertheless, Du Bois probably and Countee Cullen among them. For some, it was easy to perceive blacks as exotic, sexually liberated creatures free of white men's cares. This dubious interest won many white patrons for a few black writers, who might not have seen publication without such tainted support, though many were at work trying to destroy this vicious black stereotype and others. In "A Century of Negro Portraiture in America" (1966), Sterling Brown isolated a few such damaging images current at the time: the Comic Negro (who cannot talk, or talks funny), the Exotic Primitive, the Contented Slave of Joel Chandler Harris's stories. To them we can add the most frightening of all, the Negro Beast described by Joseph Gobineau and portrayed in such films as *Birth of a Nation,* a creature of fierce appetites and lust, usually guided by northern whites (or Reds). In his essay "The New Negro" (1925), which promoted the idea of a new Negro race consciousness, as well as Pan-Africanism, scholar Alain Locke wrote, half to present this change and half to inspire it, that "the day of 'aunties,' 'uncles,' and 'mammies' is equally gone. Uncle Tom and Sambo have passed on. . . . In the very process of being transplanted, the Negro is being transformed."

Looking back, we see that Locke's pronouncement was at least half-right. The 1920s were a time of creating images aimed at achieving new racial understanding. Several reasons are often cited for the failure of this ambitious project: the Great Depression; the inability of black writers in the 1920s to understand fully the nature of the changes they were calling for; their inability (according to Harold Cruse) to formulate a black cultural ideology, as later happened in the 1960s; and the appropriation of black material and talent by well-meaning white authors such as Carl Van Vechten, who, despite his encouragement of black writers, still saw blacks as most true to themselves when they were most unlike white men. These are historical reasons for the failure of the Harlem Renaissance; I would submit a philosophical one: namely, the inherent difficulty in trying to control the image—meaning—in the first place. Except in the case of mathematical objects, or experiences known *a priori,* we find meaning in flux, on the side of Heraclitus (change) and not Parmenides (stasis); we find, I am saying, the black world *overflowing* with meaning, so rich and multisided that literally anything—and everything—can be found there, good and bad, and one of the first chores of the writer is to be immersed in this embarrassment of rich, contradictory material. But we are not yet ready to discuss this question fully.

Although brief, the Harlem Renaissance is notable for the frequent return of some of its writers to black folk sources, a wellspring of creativity and perhaps the only truly indigenous American folklore that reached full flower in Jean Toomer's highly sophisticated, perennially hypnotic book, *Cane* (1923), a montage of poetry and short fiction. And in Zora Neal Hurston's *Their Eyes Were Watching God* (1937), a book remarkable for its beautiful use of southern folk material and its emphasis on the complex relation between black men and women—clearly, this novel and Hurston's ground-breaking anthropological work in *Mules and Men* (1935) provide the platform and the framework for black feminist writing in the 1980s. In them we see prefigured the work of Toni Morrison, Alice Walker, and such younger talents as Amirh Bahari; yet one walks away from Hurston amazed by how thoroughly she treated this (now) popular subject almost fifty years ago, using the most interesting Harlem Renaissance ideas—the importance of the common folk—to explore the "New Negro" female on subtler levels than her contemporaries did. In short, Hurston was not only a brilliant writer but also a prophetic one, a full half-century ahead of her time on questions of sexual politics. With George Schuyler's wonderful (in idea, not execution) science-fiction novel *Black No More* (1931) and Wallace Thurman's *The Blacker the Berry* (1929), the Harlem Renaissance closed with novels of black satire, books that foreshadow the barbed fiction of Ishmael Reed.

The depression, though it saw this remarkable output dwindle, gave birth to the Federal Writers' Project, which offered creative outlets to a younger generation that would become major writers in the 1940s and 1950s—Richard Wright, Ralph Ellison, Frank Yerby, Willard Motley. The role of the Communist party figures largely in this period. Earlier, Locke suggested that smarter blacks of the 1920s were leaning left with other progressive elements in America, but the thematization of blacks in American labor had been present in the late 1800s in the writings of T. Thomas Fortune, and for Du Bois, early in his career. Nevertheless, as one old organizer once told me, joining the Party was simply "something everybody did." Wright and such celebrities as Paul Robeson attracted others to the Party, but blacks were largely interested, if I'm not mistaken, in communism's promise of racial equality rather than in wholeheartedly embracing dialectical materialism and abolishing private property. On black literature, Wright's *Native Son*, an overnight bestseller in 1940, left a large artistic impression. Probably it is one of the two or three best-known novels by black American writers, and it produced many imitators but also a reaction against the brutal "realism" (if we may call it that) of his fiction during and after the depression years, a realism that gained its visceral power at the expense of portraying positive cultural features in black life—in other words, much that is affirmative and joyful in black culture is lost in the literary Lifeworld of Richard Wright.

But it *is* with Wright that something of a watershed is reached in black fiction. Nearly fifty years after its publication, *Native Son* still remains one of our most phenomenologically successful novels, a nightmare as frightening, in its own way, as George Orwell's *1984.* I am at a loss to number all the black authors who were inspired by this work. James Baldwin, Chester Himes, John A. Williams—a full generation of writers, we are forced to say, because as Baldwin once remarked, Wright's "great forte . . . was an ability to convey inward states by means of externals." What I take him to mean by this—or what he should be saying—is that for the first time in black American literature we are presented with a masterfully drawn *Lebenswelt;* we are made to see and experience meaning—the world—from the distorted perspective of a petty thief so mangled by oppression in its many forms that his only possibility for creative action is murder. Like any fully orchestrated, over-rich work of art, *Native Son* resists easy description. It is multi-leveled, exhaustive in detail, layered with existentialist, Marxist, and even religious themes; it echoes Dostoyevsky's *Crime and Punishment* and Dreiser's *An American Tragedy,* conjures the image of Nat Turner, and anticipates the thesis of Frantz Fanon in *The Wretched of the Earth* (1961) as Bigger Thomas finds release from fear and self-hatred through murder. It achieves, in the end, a dimension bordering on racial mythology (the hunt for the killer-slave), yet *Native Son* remains more than anything else a phenomenological description of the black urban experience. Wright forces us to ask, "What is it like to be thoroughly manipulated by others?" He shifts from historical details of black poverty in Chicago to a startling use of poetry and metaphor—the white world, the racial Other, is presented to Bigger's ravaged consciousness as a natural force like snow, or a blizzard, or a storm; he projects himself into innumerable objects littering the black wasteland of his family—for example, the rat killed in the opening scene—and sees his guilt in the red-hot furnace where he has placed Mary Dalton's decapitated body. Page after page, we are forced to *interpret* everyday phenomena from Bigger's unsteady position in the world, a position of powerlessness, of Pavlovian reactions to whites who are godlike but "blind" to his inner life and humanity, a position where black life is experienced as being predestined for tragedy. On yet another level, the "world" of *Native Son* is that of Greek tragedy, and for this I use John M. Anderson's definition:

"The hero [of tragedy] symbolizes participation in a process dominated by what is alien to him";[3] all one must do is replace the gods of Sophocles with modern gods who hide behind such names as "social forces" and "conditioning."

What Wright achieved in *Native Son,* and what no American writer has done quite so well since (including Wright), was the construction of a consistent, coherent, and complete racial universe—Southside Chicago—that is fully shaped by a sensitive if seared black subjectivity. Every prop on the stage of this sustained, brutal thriller refers *back* to Bigger's mind, to his special, twisted way of seeing. Nothing is neutral. Everything is charged by the broken heart and broken mind of a black boy reduced to a state of thinghood. Everything *means* something; every physical, historical object is a metaphor for feeling. Notice the ontology of Bigger's world. It is Manichean. To *be* is to be white. The Daltons' world is pure Being, a plenum, filled to overflowing with its own whiteness, while Bigger's world has a weedlike contingency—is, in fact, relative being. (Yet the alien white world's ways of seeing are *within* Bigger, like a knot in his belly.) This is Plato's world of the Divided Line and the Cave. Furthermore, Bigger is *stained* (sin) by a black body the coloration of which suggests defilement. And his world before the murder is strangely ahistorical, a shadow realm outside time. If *Native Son* is about anything, it is about the drama of consciousness itself, the effort of this boy to come fully aware of the meaning of his life and those around him. We see the "facts" of black Chicago life for the poor in the 1930s: Wright is meticulous with sociological details; he absorbs the information provided by other authors about political and economic disenfranchisement. The book "teaches." But more important than all this reportage is the fact that Wright reminds us through his method here—eidetic description, or presenting things in their lived essence (meaning) for a historical subject—that the world we live in is, first and foremost, one shaped by the mind. A writer reads him with awe. Nowhere does he cheat by resorting to narrative summary, or "telling," when a full, dramatic scene is required to show Bigger's character in and through action. Indeed, the relentless pace of *Native Son* is fueled precisely because most of the book is unmediated scene, as in a play. We see everything. We are forced to be witnesses to every thought and emotion of a national tragedy two centuries in the making. More: it is *we* whom Wright turns into murderers. Wright is shrewd, very cunning as a craftsman, using various forms of repetition (we are forced to review uneasily the details of Mary's murder at least twenty times as that awful event resurfaces in Bigger's mind) to reinforce the novel's dominant impression in a welter of details about race, class, and sexuality. Every writer dreams of achieving this, I believe—a fictional world so fully rendered that even a single glove, as Prosper Mérimée once said, has its theory and reinforces the unifying vision, the truth, of the novel as a whole.

The completeness of Wright's *Native Son* left black writers with the alternatives of repeating that vision in their fiction or grappling again with the perceptual flux of experience that characterizes the black world—and all worlds—to originate new meaning. This, indeed, was the direction taken, and grandly realized, in Ralph Ellison's *Invisible Man* (1952), which has become something of the modern Ur-text for black fiction. Ellison is indebted to Wright for certain themes (blindness, invisibility) and even, I suspect, for certain characters (his Vet greatly resembles the madman in Bigger's cell in book three of *Native Son*); but Ellison conceives his novel in an exuberant Hegelian spirit that traces a nameless black student from one "posture" of twentieth-century black life to another in prose both bewitching and (at times) prolix. And, as if this were not enough, he gives our age a new metaphor for alienation. Every chapter is structured according to the principle of "rising conflict to resolution." The book brims with stylish set pieces: the eviction scene in which every object reveals black history; Ras's monologue to Todd Clifton, which captures the essential thought of Black Nationalism; and allusions to James Joyce's *Portrait of the Artist as a Young Man,* Sigmund Freud, Booker T. Washington, and concerns spanning the Harlem Renaissance and the years following it. Almost everything one could want in a novel or vision is here: humor, suspense, black history from which Ellison's vivid imagination teases forth truth beneath mere facts, and a rogues' gallery of grotesques—Ellison is, one must admit, a sort of intellectual cartoonist when it comes to characterization; his people are, for the most part, principles.

If one must find faults with Ellison's masterpiece, they would be the artistic flaws often found in first novels. His many characters lack individual psychological realism and depth. Their vividness derives from what they represent. Nevertheless, one cannot feel terribly much, for example, about the police slaying of Todd Clifton because really no *one* has died, only the idea of "slipping outside history," which Clifton represents. Like Ellison's people in general, including his protagonist, he is a caricature without a biographical sketch, without background, without the dimensionality we expect in "rounded" characters, and Ellison admits this when he writes, "The blood ran like blood in a comic-book day in a comic-book world." At times, *Invisible Man's* allegorical level weighs a bit heavily on the story, which becomes top-heavy with symbols (all heaped into the narrator's briefcase, which is itself a symbol from the "Battle Royal" sequence). And Ellison pads out many chapters, milks them, really, with lyricism as a way of marking time when the action slows down or when connections between episodes are tenuous. An example of this would be the moment when his protagonist is released from the factory hospital and the novel structurally breaks in half. Hitherto, his protagonist has been propelled from incident to incident, from Norton to Bledso to Emerson to Liberty Paints, but now he stands directionless on a Harlem street until Mary Rambo, out of the goodness of her heart, takes him in. Or, put differently, the missing chapter called "Out of the Hospital and Under the Bar," if Ellison's editor had included it, would have provided a smoother, energetic flow between chapters eleven and twelve. Also, one must say that *Invisible Man* is a one-idea book that works its magic by carefully unpacking its central idea that meaning cannot be fixed, that Being is formless, a field of imagination and possibility that defies intellectual systemization; and by using Freudian references to the subconscious to demolish first the nineteenth-century bourgeois myths created by Booker T. Washington, then other naive optimisms of the Industrial Age, and at last the twentieth-century belief in collective action (the Brotherhood, I mean, though Ellison does seem faintly sympathetic to Pan-Africanism as symbolized by Ras) as a panacea for social ills. In this dramatized thesis, Ellison is playing with philosophical fire. But as startling as this faintly existential idea is when powerfully presented in the Rinehart section, Ellison gets the point wrong, or backward: it is not reality or the world that is formless and fluid but human perception—consciousness itself that allows us infinitely to perceive meaning as a phenomenon of change, transformation, and process; it is Mind (the subject pole of experience), not Matter (the object pole), that gives the perceived world a polymorphous character.

At bottom, *Invisible Man* is an outstanding rebellion against all forms of "authority," all "fathers"; against anything that limits Ellison's idea of freedom as equaling the lack of restraints. It is, in a way, the ultimate protest novel. Sadly, though, it leaves his protagonist nowhere to go except outside the lives of others, below the social world, which he lives off parasitically. Even sadder, this primary metaphor—invisibility—seems to force Ellison into a corner where our links to predecessors and contemporaries have been shattered. True, in the epilogue Ellison reaffirms the "principles" of *The Republic,* or plays with such reaffirmation for a paragraph, but the idea hasn't been dramatically earned. Yet, having said all this, I must add that *Invisible Man* is, as critic Roger Sale puts it, one of those rare books that cannot be ignored, and which, I believe, provided an artistic direction for black writing in the 1970s.

The other direction was offered by the Black Arts Movement, a child of Negritude (or at least its first cousin) and Cultural Nationalism.

In her article "The Black Writer and His Role," which appeared in the anthology *The Black Aesthetic* (1972), Carolyn F. Gerald writes:

> I can hold a rose before you; the image of that rose is mirrored in your eyes; it is a real image. Or I can describe a rose for you, and my words will create an image which you can visualize mentally. Perhaps you will even imagine the smell and the feel; the words I choose and the way I build them into the image are evoked, until well-defined patterns of associations based upon sensory perceptions pervade in a very vague way the whole of a man's experience.

Gerald argues that blacks, surrounded by works created by the racial Other, encounter a zero image of themselves and that a program for black cultural reconstruction is required to create positive images. Her article points out important questions of morality and value, for the image as part of our store of knowledge gives form to present perceptual experience and guides anticipation, projection into the future, plans, actions. "The artist, then, is the guardian of image: the writer is the myth-maker of his people." Gerald's insight is fine as far as it goes. It provides an interesting phenomenological foundation for a literary program, but such a program is by no means new. Image control has been the aim of black fiction—and perhaps its problem—from the very beginning of black literary production and was sounded as a specific goal, as noted earlier, during the Harlem Renaissance. Correctly, the Harlem Renaissance writers understood the image to be a workshop of meaning and perhaps even understood that the first step in treating social corruption is treating the corruption of consciousness. Their original concern with reenvisioning the lived black world touches on the dogged, very noble belief that black people, by virtue of their position in society, are somehow privy to perceptions valuable, even crucial, for fully understanding the structures of the social world. But, after critiquing the images created by the racial Other, after posing the question of black being and language, how do we "guard" the image (or meaning)? Looking back, we see the Harlem Renaissance as a tremendously productive period, and from it emerged such truly important talents as Claude McKay, whose poem "If We Must Die" is a lasting expression of man's determination to endure, one quite as good as, say, William Ernest Henley's "Invictus." But the Harlem Renaissance writers did not so much promote the efflorescence of meaning in black literature and life as they replaced old stereotypes with new ones. In order to consider a more methodological attempt at controlling meaning, it might be helpful to give a furtive glance at the esthetic "philosophy" called Negritude.

The concept of Negritude was developed in the years between 1934 and 1948 by Léopold Sédar Senghor and Aimé Césaire, who were, as it turned out, admirers of Claude McKay. With Leon Damas they founded the journal *L Étudiant Noir* and nurtured a literary movement memorable for its attempt to give authenticity to a unique African personality. Writing in "The Psychology of the African Negro" (1959), Senghor asserted that "Negro reason . . . is not, as one might guess, the discursive reason of Europe, *reason through sight,* but *reason through touch. . . ."* He added, "European reason is analytic through utilization; Negro reason is intuitive through participation." Finally, he stated that "the African Negro reacts more easily to excitements; he espouses naturally the rhythm of the object. This sensual feeling of *rhythm* is one of his specific characteristics."

For Senghor, "Emotion was Negroid," and by emotion he meant a sympathetic, even magical grasp of the world. Generally speaking, this is the spirit, or *élan,* of Negritude. According to Janheinz Jahn in *Neo-African Literature* (1966), the term "Negritude" broadly covered several meanings: (1) It was to be an instrument for liberation. (2) It was an incantatory approach to poetry that called forth the essence of things. (3) It was more often the style, feeling, and vision of a poetical work than its content. (4) It was rhythm sprung from deep emotion and feeling states, and from humor. (5) It was sympathy in contrast to understanding. (6) It was the self-affirmation of blackness. (7) It was also skin coloration and the shared experience of oppression. And finally, (8) it was the *élan* of African civilization. Obviously, these ideas presuppose what they are supposed to explain. Africa, for example, is not a homogeneous culture, and it has its own history of oppression; it is, rather, a diverse ensemble of cultures. Oppression is shared across racial lines, involving, among others, the Jews of Europe and native Americans. Skin coloration cannot be regarded as a criterion, for among Indians, both American and Hindu, and Orientals, dark pigmentation is also found Sympathetic feeling, far from distinguishing the African personality from that of the European (equated with reason, analysis), is noetic—that is, feeling states, as Heidegger demonstrates in *Being and Time,* are not easily counterpoised to reason, which also bears an affective tone *(Begriffsgefühl).*[4] What we have in Negritude, I suspect, is an inversion of black typifications derived from earlier white stereotypes. What is interesting in Senghor's explanation is that his dualism is almost Cartesian at times. He equates consciousness, *res cogitantes,* with Europe and the disembodied mind while he equates the body and its vegetable and mineral processes with Africa. He assumes racial essences that are timeless and ahistorical; in fact, for Senghor, black people seem to be less historical beings than metaphysical types.

Yet if Negritude is found wanting, it was nevertheless a well-intended effort to correct destructive racial images. The primary aim was to profile the African personality as spiritual. The African universe, according to Negritude, is full of "forces," one of which is man. A hierarchy exists, laddering forces such that at the apex is a supreme force, and below this supreme force are others of lesser efficacy that serve as intermediaries between man and God. Comparing the Afro-American concept of "soul" to Negritude, Stephen Henderson, in *The Militant Black Writer in Africa and the United States* (1969), says that both emphasize intuition, dance, the power of words, wholeness, and harmony. However, that emphasis on communalism and anti-individualism, if we look hard enough at it, trivializes the role of the very person Negritude wishes to elevate. Negritude's theory of "forces" is fairly close to the doctrine of Neoplatonism, such that the African Lifeworld is vibrant with divinity. There's really nothing wrong with this. But it is not philosophy. We have a doctrine, not analysis. My own feeling leads me to believe that Negritude's failure is the failure of all Kitsch. In *The Meaning of Modern Art,* philosopher Karsten Harries defines Kitsch this way: "In dread of freedom man pretends that the meanings with which he has endowed the world transcend their creator."[5] Surely everyone can see that the situation most characterizing our age is the fact that everything, even God, has been reduced since the Cartesian revolution to an *object* for the ego. Nothing can *be* an object unless it be for consciousness, a perceiving subject, which means the world and everything in it bears our own face, our limits, dreams, hopes. Yet Harries writes, "Unlike most modern art, which betrays the precariousness of its project, Kitsch seems to be sure of itself. Kitsch pretends to be in possession of an adequate image of man. Most modern art is too self-conscious to be that confident. . . ." Harries argues that it is precisely a lack of clarity about the world's meaning that grounds one's freedom. "To be free," he says, "is to be capable of determining, at least to some extent, what one is to be." Like fascist art in Germany during the 1930s, Negritude—all Kitsch—is a retreat from ambiguity, the complexity of Being occasioned by the conflict of interpretations, and a flight by the black artist from the agony of facing a universe silent as to its sense, where even black history (or all history) must be seen as an ensemble of experiences and documents difficult to read, indeed, as an experience capable of inexhaustible readings. But Negritude, in one incarnation or another, as one answer to the problem of controlling meaning, still exerts in the 1980s a strong influence on contemporary black literary production.

Amiri Baraka (LeRoi Jones) is perhaps the most important single figure in contemporary black arts and letters for the theoretical development of Negritude after Cesaire and Senghor. It is this remarkably talented man who in "black writing," an article among his social essays in *Home* (1966), says:

> I think though that there are now a great many young black writers in America who do realize that their customary isolation from the mainstream is a valuable way into any description they might make of America. In fact, it is just this alienation that should serve to make a very powerful American literature, since its hypothetical writers function in many senses within the main structure of the American society as well. The Negro, as he exists in America now, and has always existed in this place (certainly after formal slavery), is a natural nonconformist. Being black in a society where such a state is an extreme liability is the most extreme form of nonconformity available. The point is, of course, that nonconformity should be put to use. The vantage point is classically perfect—outside and inside at the same time. Think of the great Irish writers—Wilde, Yeats, Shaw, Synge, Joyce, O'Casey, Beckett, etc.—and their clear and powerful understanding (social as well as aesthetic) of where they were and how they could function inside

and outside the imaginary English society, even going so far as teaching the mainstreamers their own language, and revitalizing it in the doing.

Baraka placed his finger perfectly on the role all "outsiders" have played in respect to a host society: "outside and inside at the same time," and thereby capable of the observations and omniscience neither group—black or white—can generate from its center. And, as Baraka knew in his earlier days, Caliban is ironically empowered to revitalize Prospero's tongue, teaching perhaps whites the secrets of their own speech and way of seeing. Yes, this is fine indeed, but this essay is early Baraka. Like many other talented writers, he was destined to endure many changes over the years that followed its publication. By 1968, in a decade full of political assassinations, an unpopular war, and a new militancy, Baraka, like many others, was thrust completely "outside" the mainstream. In the weird, self-flagellating days of the 1960s, the dominant themes in black arts and letters were paranoia and genocide. The "evidence" for a black American holocaust seemed irrefutable. On the historical side, three centuries' worth of grim documentation, new histories such as those of Stanley M. Elkins and Eugene Genovese drove home the sense that black history was, and might always be, a slaughterhouse—a form of being characterized by stasis, denial, humiliation, dehumanization, and "relative being." Toomer had died in anonymity, an underpublished writer living out his last years in a rest home. Ellison was silent. Both Wright, in self-exile in France, and DuBois, who became a citizen of Ghana after almost a century of struggling for civil rights, had given up on America. It isn't difficult to see why. Children were dynamited in black churches, militants and pacifists both were murdered in their sleep, or blown off balconies, or set up by the FBI. It was a period when John A. Williams, in *The Man Who Cried I Am,* could write powerfully of the secret "King Alfred plan" to contain blacks during riots; when in Chicago the Black People's Topographical Library held back-room lectures (no whites allowed) on how in most cities blacks were concentrated in ghettos alongside broad freeways and through which ran railroad lines that would be used by government troops and tanks to seal us off during the "long, hot summers"; when Sam Greenlee's clumsily written *The Spook Who Sat by the Door* (1969) became the most unexpected bestseller of the early 1970s because, as one friend told me, young blacks read it to gain recipes for insurrection. (That same friend's leg was blown up—so the story was related to me—when he attempted to plant a homemade bomb in the administration building at the college we attended.) Every new incident, every experience reinforced the idea that if we stayed in America, if the old order of oppression could not be changed, we would one day again be in chains. My African friends, I learned, lived (and still live) in fear that recolonization of the African continent was just around the corner. For a young writer, these political and literary changes, which were often more symbolic than substantive, produced vertigo: that old standby periodical, *Negro Digest,* a forum for fiction and essays, transmogrified into *Black World,* and hardly an issue passed that did not feature a proponent of either Black or Cultural Nationalism. If one had even the slightest concern, or sensitivity, or distaste for injustice, one could not help being caught up in this confusion, the polarization of black and white, young and old, middle class and poor. The pressure to write "politically" was (and still is) tremendous, though little of this fiction survives today, its character—I know from experience—being less that of enduring art than that of journalism hastily written at the front, hammered out in reaction to fast-breaking (bad) news. The age produced, if you will, a new racial melodrama, or recycled the old ones of the nineteenth century with a new cast: racist spider-bellied cops, noble revolutionaries. You know this crew. No question that some black authors held fast during those trying years to produce balanced, responsible, well-crafted fiction that revealed both life's failures and its triumphs, but the air we breathed was too thick with pain for careful fiction to move center stage—as philosopher William Earle once wrote in *Public Sorrows and Private Pleasures,* "Who has the wind to shout a *qualified* thought?"[6] And one of the most powerful literary voices that reached our constantly ringing ears was Amiri Baraka's.

Theodore R. Hudson explains in *From LeRoi Jones to Amiri Baraka* (1973) that in Harlem, Baraka was instrumental in founding the Black Arts Repertory Theatre and School. Earlier, in 1927, Alain Locke had argued in "The Negro and the American Theatre" that the future of black theater was in the folk play, which expressed the beauty and colorful aspects of black life. But the essay "The Black Arts Movement" (1968) by Larry Neal, one of the most highly respected theoreticians of the 1960s, indicates some forty years later that the perception of the Negro had changed, and so had his drama. Neal identified Baraka as the prime mover behind this new theater, a theater obligated above all else to *teach.* Baraka's theater was to be owned and operated only by black people. Although the theater later failed, Baraka was well on his way to immersing himself in the Black Power struggle of the late 1960s and formulating key ideas for the Black Arts Movement, its literary sister.

Baraka moved into Newark politics, established Spirit House, and developed a close relationship with Ron Karenga, then head of the militant, nationalist self-defense organization called US. (They were brought together as early as 1967 at San Francisco State College.) For Karenga, in his essay "Black Cultural Nationalism" (1968), black art was part of the revolutionary machinery of change. It was to be judged on two levels—the social and the artistic—and for Karenga the social was primary. Technical innovation and linguistic inventiveness he considered superfluous. He argued that black art must be (1) functional, (2) collective, and (3) committed. It must "expose the enemy, praise the people, and support the revolution." Clearly, Karenga's art is agitprop and Kitsch. There are enormous problems with the apparently deathless idea that art must be "useful," especially useful to some passing social or political trend, and that it is only, as Karenga once said, "everyday life given more form and color." This is wrong. This is patently false, and I repeat these embarrassing ideas not to hold Karenga up to ridicule but only to trace to its source—or run into the ground—a form of silliness that spoils too many discussions of black fiction. Art is not *useful* in the sense that a commodity is useful (though publishers and movie producers are inclined, as they must be, to treat it as such), and art has no business begging for approval or acceptance on these terms. Although Sartre claims in *What Is Literature?* that words can be picked up by desperate men and used as a neutral tool or weapon, which is the thought behind Karenga's idea, and behind all nationalist art, the truth is otherwise: we live in language. It works upon us as we upon it—like the presence of another person before us, which in fact it, as a work of consciousness, indirectly is. The work of art raises around itself a special esthetic attitude, or intention of listening in which we momentarily leave the Natural Attitude of utility.

Nevertheless, throughout the late 1960s and the 1970s Baraka seemed indefatigable, the busiest black lecturer, teacher, and organizer in memory, and more will undoubtedly have been added to his unique story by the time you read this. My own contact with Baraka has, regrettably, been limited to the auditorium, but I must admit that no other speaker has moved me quite so thoroughly. Flanked by guards wearing dashikis (this in 1969), Baraka read poetry—sang it, really—

that was intended to indict, arouse, and incite his audience, which it did; he answered no questions from whites; he urged young black artists to bring their talent back to the black community and, leaving, carried away the breath of the young, impressionable audience with him. He acquired dozens of black imitators. In Newark he organized the Black Community Development and Defense Organization, and his efforts eventually aided the election of black mayor Kenneth Gibson.

Baraka's ever-evolving work includes numerous plays; collections of poems and essays and stories; a novel, *The System of Dante's Hell* (1966); political tracts and essays such as "A Black Value System" (1970); and propaganda plays such as *A Black Mass* (1969), in which he uses the Nation of Islam's myth of Yacub to explain the origin of the white race and describes time as a European invention. With Larry Neal he co-edited the controversial 1968 anthology *Black Fire* (recalling the Harlem Renaissance magazine *Fire*), which profiled the new black esthetics. It is Baraka, I believe, who for the most part established the style of Cultural Nationalist poetics in the period between 1960 and 1970—for an entire generation of writers, though his thought moves some distance from Negritude, drawing heavily at times on the Marxist critique of culture and economics, and occasionally from Wittgenstein in a few of his esthetic arguments. By *some* standard, Baraka is a genius. There is from the very beginning a tension in his thought between modern leftist intellectualism and race politics, between international Marxism and black nationalism—a classic conflict described by Cruse, by Wright in his autobiographical *American Hunger* (1977), and by Ellison; it is Du Bois's famous problem of the Negro who "ever feels his twoness—an American, a Negro; two souls, two thoughts, two unreconciled strivings; two warring ideals in one dark body, whose dogged strength alone keeps it from being torn asunder." The sense of black literature since the 1960s, what it means for a literary work to be socially relevant, owes much to Baraka and his followers, and we shall not be free of this art-as-weapon conception for some time. Thousands of black writers breathed the politico-esthetic atmosphere of the 1960s, a field in which Baraka was very visible as one of the angriest, most charismatic black writers; and elements of that field are still discernible in the work of younger poets and writers—male and female—working toward control of images and meaning in the 1970s and even into the 1980s. We see the influence of its odd anti-intellectualism in the late, gifted poet Henry Dumas, who eschews thought and reflection for the immediacy of feeling:

I flew into the country of the mind
And there my wings froze.
I fell.
Thought sculpted me in stone.

Dumas was, or worked at being, a mythologist. He embraced, as Carolyn Rodgers wished, African values as interpreted by Western blacks and used them to evoke a world in which everything is an essence, not existence. Objects and others, as in medieval allegorical art, *are* their names and meanings. Poet Michael Harper's views are related to Negritude's emphasis on spirituality as well, but for Harper, in his interview in *Interviews with Black Writers* (1973), the term "modality" (made to function in both a musical and a metaphysical way) best describes the Real:

> Modalilty assumes many things which society has not fully understood, although there are singular members of the society who do accept them. Number one is that man is basically spiritual. Second is that one has a "holistic" concept of the universe. This means that the universe is not fragmented, that man has a place in it, that man is a reflection of the environment, and that the environment is a reflection of man. John Coltrane was a modal musician.

For many of the post-1960s writers, the black musician is, possibly, closer to the Real than the writer is. In Dumas's story "Will the Circle Be Unbroken?" (1966), the musician Probe plays music so indigenous to the black world that it kills white members of the audience. Improvisation and spontaneity, which supposedly express feelings as they occur, are taken to be fundamental to African music and the African personality.

Black music, these thinkers argued, developed improvisation, encouraged audience participation (call-response patterns), and remained linked to functional and religious occasions. Where music was a "thing" in the West, fixed and made permanent by a text, in the black world it is short-lived deliberately, unrepeatable, and the product of spontaneity. (See, for example, Ishmael Reed's *Mumbo Jumbo,* where a search occurs for what is called "The Text," which is destroyed at the novel's end, thereby liberating man. One must also mention here James Baldwin's short story "Sonny's Blues" [1957], with its triumphant conclusion that fuses jazz, character, and racial as well as spiritual redemption in a single, masterfully evoked scene when the narrator's brother, Sonny, plays in a Harlem nightclub.) Such modern jazz musicians as Ornette Coleman, Cecil Taylor, John Coltrane, Sonny Rollins, and Sun Ra were paradigmatic artists for the cultural-nationalist writers. In this connection, one black writer even argued for the "destruction of text" in poetry. By this was meant that, although a poem was written on the page, it was not to be permanently fixed; from one reading to the next, the poem was to be deliberately altered, changed to accommodate the poet's shifting moods and those of the audience, which "participated" in the poem's spontaneous creation.

To sum up, black writers are concerned with the meaning of the black world, and this concern in literature and life has led to the creation of various racial ideologies for the African experience. In a strange way, these ésthetics are seamless. They are founded on what seems at first blush a non-European theory of man, Nature, and social life, although this soon shows itself to be deceptive, insofar as European philosophies are diverse, some involving process (Whitehead) and a nonfragmentary sense of Being. There is an almost point-by-point correspondence among esthetics, social theory, and the conception of humanity here; but let us come down to cases: the problem with all this is that it is ideology. While ideology may create a fascinating vision of the universe, and also fascinating literary movements, it closes off the free investigation of phenomena. The many elements in the mix of any ideology (for example, the notion of communalism) are often unanalyzed or rest on appeals to faith or authority or one of the several logical fallacies, and the meanings of such crucial terms are seldom defined with precision. Such esthetics are beyond critical analysis, for they are, if nothing else, fervently held forms of belief. Finally, while philosophical inquiry is devoted to understanding, a process that may or may not lead to political change, ideology must ever be geared toward action, making the reader *do* something.

And from a phenomenological perspective something very peculiar happens to consciousness with Cultural Nationalism. In his essay "The Primeval Mitosis" (1968), Eldridge Cleaver broached the stereotype of black American physicality by checking his own feelings against this myth and concluded, "The gulf between the Mind and Body will be seen to coincide with the gulf between the two races." Cleaver, focusing on one aspect of our lived experience of the body, the psychophysical, claimed that blacks were stripped of a mental life, leaving them only a bodily existence in the West—the *way* blacks are culturally intended by whites—though this bodily existence is a superior one. He assigns blacks the name "The Supermasculine Menial." And he writes, "The body is tropical, warm, hot; Fire! It is soft, pleasing to the touch, luscious to the kiss. The blood is hot. Muscles are strength." Alienated from this sensuous profile of the body, whites are characterized by Cleaver as "The Omnipotent Administrator." Weakness, frailty, cowardice, effeminacy, decay, and impotency are profiles associated with the white man's situation of abstraction from the body. Obviously, these are crude, broadly drawn outlines of our experience of the body, but Cleaver's remarks are often echoed in many black folktales that present the sexual or physical prowess of black males and in Fanon's statement in *The Wretched of the Earth* that "there are times when the black man is locked into his body," or the physical.

In my own essay "The Primeval Mitosis: A Phenomenology of the Black Body" (1976), I attempt to develop Cleaver's idea by tracing its origins to the Cartesian bifurcation of *res cogitantes* and *res extensae,* and of course to the more primordial Platonic dualism, indicating how Western ontological divisions between higher (spirit) and lower (body) coupled with Christian symbologies for light and dark develop the black body as being in a state of "stain." "The Negro suffers in his body quite differently from the white man," Fanon wrote, and this is so insofar as we have attributed to blacks the contents that white consciousness itself fears to contain and confront: bestiality, uncleanliness, criminality, all the purported "dark things." In R. W. Shufeldt's *The Negro, a Menace to Civilization* (1907) and Thomas Dixon, Jr.'s *The Leopard's Spots* (1902), the idea is extended to include black blood, which carries the germ of the underworld and the traits of lower orders of animals; one drop of black blood, for example, will cause a white family to revert to Negroid characteristics even after a full century; the mulatto, though possessing white blood, is depicted as dangerous precisely because his "outside," not being stained, betrays the criminality and animality of his interior.

And consider the concern black people of earlier generations had with body complexion, "brightening the race" through careful marriage, the terrible importance of fair skin, curly hair, and "yellah women." They were not fools, those old folks; they knew what they experienced—and understood skin-bleaching creams and straightening combs as important because these changed their stained "outsides," by which, in this social system, the depth of their "insides" would be gauged by others. (Indeed, Robert Bone has called Christianity in James

Baldwin's *Go Tell It on the Mountain* [1953] a "spiritual bleaching cream.") Stain recalls defilement, symbols of guilt, sin, corpses that contaminate, menstruating women; and with them come the theological meanings of punishment, ostracism, and the need to be "cleansed."

Black literature abounds with faintly Hegelian variations on the phenomenon of the black body as stained. Once you are so one-sidedly seen by the white Other, you have the option of (A) accepting this being seen from the outside and craftily using the "invisibility" of your interior to deceive, and thus to win survival as the folk hero Trickster John does in the "Old Marster and John" cycle. In this case, stain is like the heavy makeup of a clown; it conceals you completely. The motto of this useful opacity is the rhyme "Got one mind for whitefolks to see/Got another one that's really me"—that is, not being acknowledged as a subject is your strength, your chance for cunning and masquerade, for guerrilla warfare; you are a spy, so to speak, in the Big House. You cynically play with the frozen intentions of whites, their presuppositions and stereotypes; you shuffle or appear lazy to avoid work, or—if you are modern—you manipulate their basic fear of you as Darkness and Brute Power to win concessions. It is what Ellison calls "Rinehartism" in *Invisible Man*. It is the tactic taken by Cross Damon in Wright's *The Outsider* (1953) when Damon, after he is freed from his former life by a train wreck and begins to construct a new identity for himself, must secure a false birth certificate and thinks, "He would have to present to the officials a Negro so scared and ignorant that no white man would ever dream that he was up to anything deceptive."

Or you may (B) seize this situation at its roots by reversing the negative meaning of the black body. "It is beautiful," you might say, "I am a child of the Sun." The situation of the black-as-body possessing noncognitive traits is not here—in Cultural Nationalism—rejected, but rather stood on its head: the meaning still issues, of course, from the white Other. You applaud your athletic, amorous, and dancing abilities, your street wisdom and *savoir faire,* your "soul," the food your body eats; you speak of the communal (single-body) social life of your African ancestors before the fifteenth-century slave trade, their bodily closeness to the earth. You are Antaeus in this persuasion of the alienated black self's phenomenological pilgrimage to itself, and the whites—flesh-starved invaders, freebooters, buccaneers, seamen who bring syphilis to ancient Alkebu-lan—are alienated physically from the earth. They see their lost humanity in you. They steal you to take it home. If you are a member of the early Nation of Islam and believe in the mythology of Yacub, the black scientist who created a "white Beast" from the black community, you intend whites as quasi men "grafted" from the original black-as-body until, by degrees, the Caucasian appears as a pale and pitiful abstraction from yourself, ontologically removed several stages from the basic reality you represent.

This control and reconstitution of images, which arises out of the noble work of counteracting cultural lies, easily slips toward dogma that ends the process of literary discovery. In short, toward Kitsch. The Black Aesthetic culminated, curiously, in a devotedness to God and Country. The god, however, is plural, manifested in all beings; and the country, regrettably, refers to a black nation-state that exists only in the minds of the nationalists. It must be said, however, that the Cultural Nationalists and image controllers wished to be—and many are—moral men and women. In his essay "Richard Wright's Blues" (1945), Ellison borrows the term "pre-individual" from critic Edward Bland to describe the black community. Bland is quoted:

> In the pre-individualistic thinking of the Negro stress is on the group. Instead of seeing in terms of the individual, the Negro sees in terms of "races," masses of people separated from other masses of people according to color. Hence, an act bears intent against him as a Negro individual. He is singled out not as a person but as a specimen of an ostracized group. He knows that he never exists in his own right but only to the extent that others hope to make the race suffer vicariously through him.

Throughout the control-of-images argument, Negritude, and Cultural Nationalism, this "pre-individualistic" tendency emerges again and again. "The pre-individualistic black," writes Ellison, "discourages individuality out of self-defense. Having learned through experience that the whole group is punished for the actions of the single member, it has worked out efficient techniques for behavior control." Obviously, it cannot be through such ideologies that genuine creative work is achieved. Rather, all presuppositions, all theories, must be suspended before experience and meaning can be brought forth in black literary art.

2

■ *Being and Fiction*

■ Henri Bergson once remarked, "I call an amateur in philosophy anyone who accepts the terms of a usual problem as they are. Doing philosophy authentically would consist in *creating* the framework of the problem and creating the solution." To a degree, this is what black literary practice must do, for it still tends to rest on shaky esthetic foundations. The same can be said of many American creative-writing courses. No, I'm not saying that writing teachers do a poor job, simply that as a young writer I wrestled with what I read and heard, in hope of getting better, and found much of it badly confused and lacking in clarity. Once again, a good example is the way we talk about experience.

Popular wisdom has it that this element—direct experience—is the raw stuff of creative writing. Most of the time we speak of experience simply as something that "happened" to us, or as what we have seen, which is okay, a harmless enough thing to do, though this kind of talk shortchanges the enormous role played by imagination and language and cultural conditioning in our perception and assumes that meaning is *given* directly to us with little or no shaping necessary from our side. It's okay to speak this way at cocktail parties, but consider how many beginning writers have shipped out on tramp steamers or risked pneumonia like Stephen Crane in open boats to accumulate "experience," as if it were a commodity, a thing we need to heap up before writing can begin. Consider how *thin* in detail and description their reports have been after they got back from their adventuring—mere travelogue, postcard stuff used for setting and props, as if they lacked proper distance from the event, saw when they were there nothing in terms of highly individualized specifics—what Gerard Manley Hopkins called inscape—or saw things selectively, but who can escape that? In other words, how many have lived with the Sandinistas, or smuggled drugs through South America, and selected all the *wrong* details? Saw, in effect, what they'd believed they'd see before leaving home, and there-fore saw nothing new at all? Sometimes this uncritical notion of experi-ence runs to silliness. Authors complain of having exhausted their store of it. Poor writers or wealthy ones are told they cannot truly cross class boundaries. Black writing rarely, if ever, attempts to reconstruct the complexity of the world as seen through the eyes of a richly detailed, three-dimensional white character, or of other nonwhites (native Amer-ican, say, or Asian), and who can doubt these days that male writers worry, as well they should, about authentically presenting a female point of view? But if I'm not mistaken, great literature resolves these problems of viewpoint and epistemology by emphasizing the fact that literary art is at its best when it is a sumptuous act of imagination, invention, and interpretation.

Because no experience is "raw." None is *given* to us as meaningful, or as meaning only one thing.

Seldom, if ever, is an isolated event or "experience" significant by itself or worthy of fictional treatment. No, its value lies in its relation to other events. Or, as E. M. Forster puts it, "to events arranged in time sequence." In *Aspects of the Novel,* a series of lectures that has deserved-ly been in print for over half a century, this is his minimalistic definition of story—lunch follows breakfast and precedes dinner, or using his own example, "The king died, and then the queen died."[1] Even so spare an account of the *eidos,* or essence, of every story is freighted with judgment, for it presents the story (which in this form can also be a newspaper article, a joke, or history) as a temporal being, an organiza-tion of before-and-after, or, in Aristotelian terms, structured with a "beginning, middle, and end." Are those structures of events in the world? Well, yes, but only to the extent that they are structures of you and me. Temporality describes *our* being, how *we* see. Even that, of course, is too sketchy. We perceive in the present only, remember the past, and project ourselves into the future, a constant flip-flopping about of mind that Edmund Husserl analyzes in *The Phenomenology of Inter-nal Time-Consciousness* and that Richard Wright adroitly exploits to generate tension in *Native Son*—that is, half the things that make Big-ger's heart wham and push the novel along are his imagined scenarios of capture and death, his habit of preliving scenes of racial torment. Though skeletal, this orderly description of the story plunges us into a pattern that says a great deal more about Western esthetic logic than, say, cultures (or modes of consciousness) less linear than our own. And by the time Forster proceeds to define "plot" by use of the example "The king died, and then the queen died of grief," we as readers have rushed boldly into the forest of hermeneutic philosophy. Here, with the introduction of causation (died of grief), events have *glue* between them, connectedness, an immaterial linkage between matter and mind, objective occurrence and subjective response: the soul and the world are one. Plot, if this traditional definition is credible, is an act of faith.

And whatever else it may be dramatically, each plot—how events happen and why—is also an *argument.* To plot well is to say, "This is how the world works," that if you place *this* person A in *this* situation B, the result will be event C. If plot is anything, it is a vehicle of reason. Or, if you prefer, high speculation on why things turn out as they do. If some writers find plot to be a difficult problem to solve, I would wager it is because they also find it difficult to engage in the ballet of argumentation, and also because they are not familiar with the many forms that reason or reasoning can assume. It is this basic, genuinely exploratory element in creative writing that leads some phenomenologists such as Maurice Merleau-Ponty to conclude that philosophy and fiction—both disciplines of language—are about, at bottom, the same business.[2] Merleau-Ponty, of course, goes farther than that, making it clear in *Sense and Non-Sense* that our lives are inherently metaphysical insofar as each moment of perception, each blink of the eye, involves the activity of interpretation; perception is an *act,* and this observation puts the lie to that ancient stupidity that says the processes of philosophy and fiction are two different enterprises—they are sister disciplines, I would say, and unless a critic realizes this, his position is simply untenable. More specific to this point of the sisterhood of fiction and philosophy is the article "Phenomenological Variations and Artistic Discovery" in philosopher Don Ihde's *Existential Technics,* where he persuasively argues that the method known as "phenomenological (fantasy) variations" performed on the phenomenon in order to exhibit its full range of meaning or profiles (*Abschattung*) is a systematic form of discovery already present in the arts. The arts, he says, are "latently 'phenomenological' in their primary use of variations." Ihde lays out these forms of variations as follows: figure-ground reversals, juxtapositions of context, the isolation of dominant and recessive characteristics, transformations of perspectives, and even deconstruction as devices used to shock and to cause disjuncture, thereby freeing perception from the familiar.[3] To this I would add another shared technique: namely, "phenomenological description" itself, the manner in which we use words, particularly in prose that is charged or poetic or surrealistic, to fling the reader of fiction toward revelation and unsealed vision.

We must now talk about language. I think I understand, at least on a gut level, the suspicion of modern writers such as Alain Robbe-Grillet that words cannot be trusted, least of all metaphors that, if scratched deeply enough, reveal bourgeois ideology, the pananthropic content of traditional humanism, and, by implication, lead to what I would call a form of interpretative imperialism closing out all other visions of Being. Many writers have broached this problem, among them the philosopher-novelist William Gass, whose elegant and entertaining essays present the question in, I believe, the liveliest manner. In "The Ontology of the Sentence," Gass invokes Aristotle to explain how "it is impossible in a discussion to bring in the actual things discussed; we use their names as symbols instead of them; and therefore we suppose that what follows in the names, follows in the things as well. . . . But the two cases (names and things) are not alike."[4] And he proceeds then to let Martin Heidegger say a few words: "What could be more obvious than that man transposes his propositional way of understanding things into the structure of the thing itself?" (But Gass, trained in the tradition of analytic philosophy, stops here to avoid the rest of Heidegger's esthetics, which presents the poet and the philosopher as commonly united in their duty to interpret Being through a Saying that Shows the essence of things.) The position we are forced ultimately to acknowledge is that words capture neither the nature of things nor the relations between them. Nature gives us no metaphors. If we pursue this thought to its logical conclusion, we must envision all thought and things to be of different species—literature, or all word makings (including today's newspaper, history, and biography), is a creation of illusions, for as Karsten Harries says, "As the world does not justify man's demands for meaning he invents an imaginary world in which he can feel at home." Like Hume in *A Treatise of Human Nature,* we must cast a suspicious eye at the very foundations of Western thought and science: the idea of personal identity, God, and even causation. The *telos* of this thought, which takes its most two-fisted form in Wittgenstein's effort to free philosophy from the "fly-bottle" of language, moves sooner or later to the dissolution of the cultural world, perhaps even to silence in art—the empty canvas, the blank page, the simple quiet sitting of John Cage at his piano. I personally have no problem with this, being an on-again-off-again Buddhist, someone who can appreciate the zen-like thrust of this argument. (The Sixth Patriarch Huineng tells us that when we see the flag blowing it is not the flag that moves, nor even the wind, as one might think, but instead only the mind of the perceiver.) And, being black, I can appreciate the sobering effect of this argument, which is the best corrective to Kitsch one can imagine. There are no "blacks," or "nations," or even "men" and "women," unless by this we mean, say, specifically my son, Malik, and my daughter, Elizabeth; but even that says little or nothing at all: one meaning of Malik is "the prince," and of Elizabeth, "consecrated to God," but have these meanings—crucial if given to a fictional character—anything whatsoever to do with the creatures running in and out of my study as I work? Not at all, except in so-called primitive cultures where a name defines a nature. They remain mysterious, ineffable, beyond language finally. In *Fiction and the Figures of Life* Gass tells us, "There are no descriptions in fiction, there are only constructions."[5] Try as I might, I cannot deliver my children, or anyone, to you through words. Though I may pile detail upon detail in a prose passage describing them, giving you their biographies, their physical descriptions, image heaped upon image, portraying them through action and, as a fully omniscient narrator, even their inner lives—despite all this, I shall never be able to describe or detail *enough* to "capture" them in words, which are merely signs or symbols bearing within themselves a concept, a meaning we have agreed on, and never the curious, unlimited thing we call a life. Gass writes, "But Mr. Cashmore is not a person. He is not even an object of perception, and nothing whatever that is appropriate to persons can be correctly said of him. There is no path from idea to sense . . . and no amount of careful elaboration of Mr. Cashmore's single eyeglass, his upper lip or jauntiness is going to enable us to *see* him." So the argument goes—the argument, I believe, of Positivists and analytic philosophers who, it's clear, have cornered the writer of fiction like a caged beast—a paper tiger, one realizes, whose claws have been clipped and whose supposed power to terrify and thrill us is now reduced to no more than a ridiculous sham. "The work," Gass claimed in a 1979 interview in the *New Republic,* "is filled with only one thing— words and how they work and how they connect." Fiction for this philosopher is "a method which, by its very nature and demands, deforms." So the writer can make, it seems, no claims that his work windows in any way onto the world of real men, real women, or real events. It can reveal nothing except its own proliferating mechanisms, feed on nothing except the fuel of its own logical possibilities as a game. How devastating a development is this idea in contemporary letters? Well, very much so. Listen to John Gardner, Gass's friendly antagonist and the author of *On Moral Fiction,* as he speaks through Martin Orrick, a character in his novel *Stillness,* posthumously published in 1986:

> The urge to make art discover truth was a childish, wrong-headed urge, as his friend Bill Gass kept crabbily insisting in article after article in *The New York Review,* as if hoping if he said it enough he'd at last grow resigned to it. Well, not Martin Orrick. It filled him with the rage of a hurt rhinoceros— though he'd admit it was true—that human consciousness had no business in the world, that the world was its relative by accident.... Writing his fiction, struggling for hours to get a gesture just right, or to translate into English the exact sound of the first large drops of an August rain on a burdock leaf, he would look up suddenly with a heart full of anger and a belly full of acid from too much black coffee, too many hours at his pipe, remembering again that all he so tirelessly struggled for was false from its engendering: he was torturously authenticating by weight of detail, by linguistic sleight-of-wit, actions that never took place on this earth since Time began and never would, never could. Nature's love stories had nothing to do with those novelists made up....

Only a fool, one gathers after reading Gass, would waste his time glancing now from the portraits on the page to the world, hoping to gauge the former by the latter—Bigger Thomas, say, by the black thief one encounters in a real Southside poolhall in Chicago, for Bigger represents no one, is, Gass must say, only a "linguistic location" modified by the rest of the four-hundred-page text. "Authors who believe they must, to move their fictions, hunt endlessly through circumstances for plausible causes as they might for them in life," Gass writes, "have badly misunderstood the nature of their art. . . ." Bigger's nature, then, is more that of the sort of entities we find in mathematics: a "universal embodied," for Gass. Numbers, for example, or more exactly, pure transcendent *meaning:* a mental construct. It is this sort of being fictional characters possess, and the proper model for the novelist is not, as one might think, the reporter or biographer, but instead the system builder or mathematician who, in a carefully wrought, coherent, internally consistent theorem, creates a beautiful architecture of meaning that may or may not have anything to do with the world of everyday experience. Probably not. "Like the mathematician," says Gass, "like the philosopher, the novelist makes things out of concepts." If not the mathematician, then let us choose Thomas Aquinas, whose *Summa Theologica*—like a good, long novel—satisfies all the requirements of coherence, consistency, and completeness, even to the degree of defining a universe where stones, men, and angels coexist in perfect harmony, where no question is unanswered by his method, where a whole picture emerges of Being. But is this *our* world? We needn't ask. It is enough that it is a highly imaginative, made-up universe of meanings that interlock seamlessly, for in this we find beauty—an object of esthetic and intellectual contemplation, one that rewards us with each revisitation. As for metaphor, well, this: it is merely a means of fastening words to one another, not words to things. It can provide, for Gass, "a consciousness electrified by beauty," and its delights are "as wide as the mind is, and musicked deep with feeling." Fiction offers us a tiny universe, a "coherent deformation of Reality," as Merleau-Ponty claims, as well as Mikel Dufrenne,[6] each novel or story or poem like a terrarium, or one of those miniature wintry scenes inside globes sold at Christmastime and that, if shaken, fill with artificial snow. That none of these universes can compete with any other gives readers the glorious option—so I would guess—of inhabiting innumerable "worlds" as they go from one book to the next. See this as a wagon wheel where you can journey out on an infinity of spokes, each different, though the wheel has no hub or center.

This sort of fiction—"linguistic sculpture," Gardner calls it in *On Moral Fiction*—will satisfy some readers, and it will please critics who do not "read" a book referentially and seek only to comprehend a literary work in terms of its internal perfection, as one might appreciate the stylized beauty of a logical proof. A "well-made" fiction *must* have this unity, but I believe Gass, who loves to be playful and provocative, has painted for us an extreme, fringe account of language and literary art in order to draw us back from naivety and nonsensical discussions about art. However, as an extreme account, it ignores the parasitic quality of language; I mean speaking as such, which siphons what sense it has from the utterances of men and women seriously trying to understand their experiences. Gass's notion of the "concept" or idea is too Platonic. Ideas—and even universals, even numbers—are historical beings, ever changing as our intention toward them changes; time and human *praxis* may even alter the sense of their relations. (We do not, I am saying, have the same sense of what numbers mean as the pre-Socratics or the creators of the *I Ching*.) It's really unimportant that

Malcolm Lowry's Mexico in *Under the Volcano* isn't Mexico; in fiction we seek not an experience of Mexico, which is nothing, or rather is so *much* in the way of perceptual experience that it is over rich, open-ended regarding its meaning, and thereby defies our understanding. No, we want our collective experiences of Mexico—what so many have said about it—brought to a greater clarity: a word picture, or conceptual presentation that bodies forth a meaning we *can* carry with us when we confront the "real" Mexico again, a meaning that is by no means final and immutable like a Platonic form. Hardly. Its meaning evolves. And so Lowry's "Mexico" adds to our gathering sense of the place, enriching the life of the spirit through language, through literature, and in no sense closes off the efflorescence of understanding.

On the most visceral level, in that place of the heart where most of us live, the majority of readers will be drawn toward Gardner's embattled belief that fiction should be "moral" and "life affirmative"; if not to Gardner, then perhaps to his idol, Leo Tolstoy, who in *What Is Art?* (1898) proposed that "art is a human activity, consisting in this, that man consciously, by means of certain external signs, hands on to others feelings he has lived through, and that other people are infected by these feelings, and also experience them"; if not to Tolstoy, then perhaps to William Faulkner's acceptance speech for the Nobel Prize in 1949, in which he claimed that it is "the problems of the heart in conflict with itself which alone can make good writing." But it is Gass who is more convincing, at least in a narrow sense. Our interest here does not lie in deciding on either view of fiction. Black writing assumes, as it must, the traditionally held correspondence between word and world (except in the work of Clarence Major), and I am going to say flat out that I don't believe this ancient faith in fiction is entirely without foundation. By angling in on the problem through phenomenology and what other poets and writers have to say, we might achieve a kind of workable middle ground.

"The language is communal, cumulative," reports William Matthews, a very fine poet as sensitive as any to language as a *lived* experience, and who adds in an interview in *Aegis*:

> Something of the life of everyone who's used language is in it. I'm thinking not only of the great literary masters, but of anyone who has ever spoken it. Babysitters, seed dealers, shepherds, anyone. The language is in circulation, as we say of money, and like money it has on it the sweat and palm oil of everyone who's used it. While I write by myself, I'm in touch, through

language, with countless others living and dead. . . . Language continues to
return a writer to the central human questions, not so much as he defines
them, but as they've been defined by those who use the language. If it does
that well, it becomes a small part of the accumulation.

The poet is saying both that the forms of artistic expression guide
and focus his feelings about what he wishes to say (as some poems, the
sonnet, for example, have proven their ability to treat questions of
appearance versus reality) and that such basic linguistic choices as
rendering an experience in short, simple sentences as opposed to
compound-complex ones, or favoring short vowels and hard consonants (instead of the reverse) *alters* both his and the reader's experience of the event. He means that in words we find the living presence of
others, that language is not—nor has it ever been—a neutral medium
for expressing things, but rather that intersubjectivity and cross-cultural
experience are already embodied in the most microscopic datum of
speech. Critic Marjorie Boulton, whom we owe a debt of thanks, makes
this evident in *The Anatomy of Poetry* (1968). She indicates that on the
level of what Aristotle once called *melos,* or the sound dimension of
language, a fledgling or a seasoned wordsmith cannot escape the fact
that connotative meaning clings to sound like ants to a sweetapple: *b* and
p sounds *feel* explosive; *m, n,* and *ng* we experience as humming and
musical; *l* as liquescent, holding within itself something of streams,
water, rest; *k, g, st, ts,* and *ch* as harsh; *t, w,* and *v* as evocative of wind,
wings, an easy light motion; *t* and *d* as best suited for short actions; and
th tends to be soothing. Emotion, relative to this culture, has *become*
sound—or, more precisely, centuries of poetic usage has sedimented
certain aural phenomena so thoroughly that we can without sounding
too foolish speak of music as being "sad" and of falling patterns of rain
off our shingles as "musical." Machinery in the age of Marx is all *b* and *p*
and *k* sounds, which helps us hate the assembly line all the more, but
software woos us with *m*'s and *l*'s. Okay . . . let us push on to something
science-fiction writer Theodore Sturgeon has raised his hand to say:

The words are pressuring you as you are pressuring the words. The
ultimate comes out as a compromise—preferably a greater compromise
than a lesser one. . . . You have to choose your words carefully to fit a
particular cadence, and that means you can't use the words you were going
to use; you have to pick other words that mean the same thing, or almost the
same thing.

It is in and through the process of fiction—the presence of others in language—that the expression Sturgeon wishes to convey gains clarity, and both he and Matthews seem comfortable in the midst of the culture(s) language enshrines. To put this bluntly, language is transcendence. And so is fiction. They comport us "other there" behind the eyes of others, into their hearts, which might make some few of us squeamish, for suddenly our subjectivity is merged with that of a stranger. On these matters, Merleau-Ponty is our best guide for making clear how great is our debt to our predecessors and contemporaries whenever we use these common cultural phenomena—language and literary form—to create fiction. Writing, Merleau-Ponty tells us in *The Prose of the World,* "is the trespass of oneself upon the other and of the other upon me. . . ."[7] Why else do we fling books into the fire if not because, in the case of great fiction, and deep within our depths, the writer is leading us in a direction we know is inevitable but toward which we sometimes *do not wish to go,* especially if it will shatter our smugness, or displace us from our fondest prejudices? To read is to inhabit the role and real place of others; to write is a stranger experience yet, for it involves a corresponding act of self-surrender such that my perceptions and experiences are allowed to coincide with those who came before me and despoiled words, shaped their sense and use, who impose the "accumulation" of sense, as Matthews puts it, upon us until my life and the life of others "intersect and engage each other like gears," according to Merleau-Ponty.

All this, to a degree, echoes Jean-Paul Sartre's famous line in *Saint Genet,* "The Word is the Other."[8] But there is a difference worth pointing out. Others frightened Sartre. In fact, *things* made Sartre edgy. Language is a *mob.* The communal dimension of language also becomes a dilemma for some contemporary black and feminist writers—becomes a lynch mob, I guess, for the Other is white. And male. Someone *not* sympathetic with their sense of things. Like a palimpsest, the word is a tissue of interpretations, but many of them male-chauvinist and bigoted. Language is the experience, the sight (broad or blind) of others formed into word. If *blue* can embody royalty, cold, sadness, infinity, the celestial, black music, tranquility, and a score of other meanings simultaneously, it is because *blue* in its fullness is a common property, like an old Baptist church, layer upon layer of sense that opens onto the antithetical vision and perspectives of our predecessors; but I would wager these are both white and black, male and female, for like everything else the language is not fixed but evolving. For all that, this theme—call it Caliban's dilemma—sometimes crackles throughout serious black fiction: the solitary black writer sitting in his or her room trying to express an "experience" is, at the very instant thought coalesces into word, thrown suddenly into the midst of a crowd, but a very integrated crowd, I might add, and what is expressed is inevitably a compromise between the one and the many, African and European, the present and the past. This will be clearer, I suspect, when we delve into the subject of character, a matter of such importance that we should turn to it immediately.

At first blush, it sounds cranky to harp at this late hour in American literary history on the priority of character. Read: the importance of people. Even armchair critics will agree that pretty much everything in first-rate fiction as well as in film, or in all narrative forms of entertainment, hinges on this matter. Nevertheless, it's an axe I shall grind again and again in discussing contemporary black American fiction because if the central characters of the story, the people, are not "developed," as popular books on writing say—if they are not "round," possessing details of biography, psychological depth, social background, eccentricities, relations to others, and reasons for being as they are, reasons we can associate with "real" people—then surely plot, which is based on the specifics of *this* person in *this* situation, cannot achieve Aristotelian *energia,* or the actualization of the potential inherent in a story; plot will seem, at best, merely *imposed* upon the characters from the outside, thereby revealing the heavy, manipulative hand of the sloppy writer-puppeteer. All this seems sound, even commonplace, provided we don't poke at it too much. But isn't it true that the moment we broach the question "Who is this character?" we instantly tumble toward a deeper, more difficult problem that is fiction's business to raise repeatedly and only provisionally to resolve: namely, what *is* a person? Or, phrased differently, what the hell do we count as convincing in the rendering of "character"?

Anyone who has associated with actors will, I suspect, see that this problem has its analogue on the stage or before the movie camera. We admire truly great actors because they have a knack for disappearing into any number of difficult roles. transforming not only their speech—grammar, voice, vocabulary, and the unique music that erupts from each human throat—but also their most personal gestures, body language, idiosyncratic tics, emotional reactions to objects and others, and, momentarily, the fundamental ways they live in the world. It has been one of the blessings of my life to study actors as they extended into performance scripts I've struggled to write over the years, and what you see most vividly in the craft of such conscientious actors as Glynn Turman, Richard Dysart, and LeVar Burton is an imaginative act that is thrilling to anyone steeped in Continental philosophy or the fictional process. On location in Texas cowtowns for my first film, a docudrama called "Charlie Smith and the Fritter Tree" (1978), Glynn Turman spent hours reviewing videotapes of Charlie Smith, who, at 137, was a former black cowboy and the oldest living American. In Smith's case, an actor had to ask, "How does a black captured in Liberia in 1848 and sold at the *cabildo* to a Texas rancher, who raised him as a cowboy, eat his soup? Engage in foreplay, or *does* he know anything about foreplay? How does he walk into a room?" Unlike so many "stars" who rely on anger and rage (the easiest emotions for an actor to play), Turman emphasized all the subtle "colors" on the continuum of expression, a palette where no pure colors exist, but instead emotion as we experience it as a complex commingling of one or more different, even contradictory emotions. He plucked from his developing portrayal of Smith the specific nine-teenth-century phrases that sometimes surfaced in the old man's speech; he studied what he did with his hands, how he held his ciga-rettes, hoisted a whiskey bottle, how he shifted his weight when stand-ing, the ways in which the inner man was bodied forth through external action, taking from Smith what were *eidetic* or essential quirks for *this* life, but also diving, in a process almost dialectical, deeper into himself, into memory for his own experiences, and those of others, that might dovetail with Smith's and thereby bring our subject into greater relief.

Being new to screenwriting at age twenty-nine, I often went skimpy on stage directions. Turman, as if picking up a torch, took my paltrier scenes imaginatively further than I'd dreamed possible, hunting for exact gestures that echoed on several levels of meaning, using his body to amplify each line of dialogue or to fill with tension the beats or silences between dialogue; he had to know—as a craftsman who cared—what he was thinking, or should be thinking, at every instant, at exactly what spot he, a slave, should stand in an antebellum farmhouse kitchen when he delivered a reply to his owner, and with what verbal and nonverbal concessions to the southern etiquette created for mas-ters and slaves. Everything for this remarkable man had to work to-gether: his precise sense of timing leading his body to turn toward the camera just as his breath came inward, then out in a final sentence that stressed the last syllable, which, like the slamming of a farmhouse door, closed the scene, relieved the emotional tension established earlier, and carried us into the scenes to follow. Watching Turman's microscopic conjuring of hundreds of imaginative, intelligent details, tic after tic, I was forced to shake off my creative slumbers; I felt the need to improve myself immediately as a writer. On the first, superficial level, I realized that, in fiction, I must combine in one person the division of labor characteristic of every film production. In fiction, especially the novel, I had to *be* every character. If a book was to have the layered quality that rewards additional readings, I had to be the director, and also the costumer, carpenter, cameraman, the hairdresser and prop person. I had to know the names for everything on the stage, which must be carefully "dressed" for each fictional scene: I had to know the specific technical words a seamstress would use in ordering materials for Turman's nineteenth-century blouse, the phrases the propman would use for Civil War currency in Turman's pocket, and the terms a house builder would employ for every part of the front door he has built for the farmhouse. And all this required, I realized, a lifetime of endless research into dozens of specialized fields. And, watching Turman, I saw another thing:

In his delicate construction of a half-real, half-imagined life I saw the delicious satisfaction, the gleeful delight skillful actors and protean novelists share, a kind of childhood pleasure that comes from being somebody else, understanding them through the canniest (and often cruelest) sort of imitation and mimicry; our finest art, it struck me, was grounded in this almost primordial sense of playacting, one shared perhaps by the tribal hunter who throws over his shoulders a wolf's pelt, performs actions he believes applicable to his prey, then hunts him the following day. And, strange to say, there was a great, self-effacing love for Smith in Turman's performance, as if the act of re-creation involved a patient listening, a bracketing of what he personally found disagreeable about the old man's values and behavior, sympathetic observation, and as much empathy as any human being could muster.

Philosophers, too, will find in the actor's and writer's crafts a phenomenological foundation, or aboriginal faith. In *The Structures of the Life-World,* Alfred Schutz tells us that it is a fundamental axiom of the social world that "if I were there where he is now, then I would experience things in the same perspective, distance, and reach as he does. And, if he were here where I am, he would experience things from the same perspective as I."[9] In other words, the actor and writer—and all of us really—believe in the interchangeability of standpoints; we throw ourselves *with* a character toward his projects, divest ourselves of our own historically acquired peculiarities, and reconstruct his world. This is, one sees immediately, difficult. And dangerous in the writer's case, for what he personally believed before writing his story—the point he wanted to make—will, in all likelihood, be severely modified. (But isn't this the very process of truth?) In effect, this method shared across fiction and the stage is a form of phenomenological "free" variation. In his essay "Phenomenology through Vicarious Experience," philosopher Herbert Spiegelberg suggests a few steps for phenomenology—or intuition of other lives—through indirect experience: (1) Using imagination and the techniques of variation, we try to occupy the real place of the other and view from this standpoint the world as it is present in all its texture, limitations, and possibilities. (2) In transporting ourselves in this manner we must divest ourselves of our own historically acquired peculiarities by adopting as much as we can of the other's viewpoint. We must quit the familiarity of our own lives momentarily to experience this. (3) After this transposition we move back and forth between the other's perspective and our own, comparing evidence, collating profiles, criticizing the other's perspective for what it lacks, and, according to what we find, amending our own.[10]

Doubters may object that it is racially impossible to strip themselves of their own historically acquired traits. Many black writers claim they cannot imagine what it is like to be white, that all they know is the "black" experience. For my money, this objection is sheer laziness. I will also say such objections are based on a very circumscribed notion of race. We can, I think, trash such objections quickly by noting that in a country as genetically mongrelized as America it wouldn't be unthinkable to scrap racial nature altogether. Anyone knowledgeable about genetics, such as Guy Murchie, can show you that if you go back fifty generations in the life of any person, he or she shares a common ancestor with every other person on this planet. None of us can be less closely related than fiftieth cousins. "Race" dissolves when we trace the gene back to A.D. 700.[11] Our lives, as blacks and whites, we come to realize, are a tissue of cross-cultural influences. One can say as much about this book, written by a black American (as Murchie might point out) on paper invented by the Chinese and printed with ink evolved out of India and from type developed by Germans using Roman symbols modified from the Greeks, who got their letter concepts from the Phoenicians, who had adapted them partly from Egyptian hieroglyphs.

What I am outlining here, by way of actors and science and history, is the enduring truth that if we go deeply enough into a relative perspective, black or white, male or female, we encounter the transcendence of relativism; in Merleau-Ponty's terms, "to retire into oneself is to leave oneself." Why is this so? Because what we have, from the standpoint of phenomenology, are not different worlds but instead innumerable perspectives on *one* world; and we know that, when it comes to the crunch, we share, all of us, the same cultural Lifeworld—a world layered with ancestors, predecessors, and contemporaries. To think of this world properly is to find that all our perspectives take us directly to a common situation, a common history in which all meanings evolve. Merleau-Ponty writes eloquently in *Adventures of the Dialectic:*

> My own field of thought and action is made up of imperfect meanings, badly defined and interrupted. They are completed over there, in the others who hold the key to them because they see sides of things that I do not see, as well as, one might say, my social back. Likewise, I am the only one capable of tallying the balance sheets of their lives, for their meanings are also incomplete and are openings onto something that I alone am able to see. I do not have to search far for the others; I find them in my experience, lodged in the hollows that show what they see and what I fail to see. Our experiences thus have lateral relationships of truth: all together, each possessing clearly what is secret to the other, in our combined functionings we form a totality which moves toward enlightenment and completion.... We are never locked in ourselves.... [12]

No, never "locked in ourselves" unless we choose to be, a choice that is suicide for a creative writer. Literature abounds with accounts of the basically "autobiographical" writer, the faintly solipsistic soul who primarily rakes through his own "experiences." Without going into the fact that such authors are constantly rewriting, editing severely, or reenvisioning their lives, or the fact that Glynn Turman's portrayal of Charlie Smith *was* Turman as well as Smith, I would like to suggest that what we damn in Johnny-one-note actors we are inclined to damn in writers, too. I mean playing only themselves in one performance after another. You get that feeling, and in a way that sickens, from Sylvester Stallone and Arnold Schwarzenegger, who are "stars" certainly, but not actors; you never get that from Dustin Hoffman, who can *be* anyone, or

Vanessa Redgrave, a talent capable of conjuring characters of either gender. Occasionally, when I wish to be grumpy, or after reading student stories in which the young writer *is* his or her character, someone mainly worried about getting laid, I ask my students, "Don't you think it's miserable to live your entire life, fifty or sixty years on this planet, and have no idea whatsoever of how someone else has suffered, what is in *their* heart, *their* hopes and fears, *their* pain and personal triumphs?" At this point, they all look at the floor, feeling nervous. Then I back off a bit, because perhaps we can never know others. Phenomenology aside, perhaps all we shall ever know are the workings of our own nervous systems. But real fiction *tries.* Its faith is that of transcendence. Like the great actor who loves people of all kinds, and enjoys being changed by them, the true novelist, the ambitious story writer, delighting in ventriloquy and dressing up like Mom and Dad (or heroes and villains) and losing himself in the rich interpretative material provided by others, delighting even in the conflict of interpretation this brings—this kind of writer is forever obliged to obliterate for the duration of his fiction his own pettiness, to surrender his prejudices in order to seize another's way of seeing, then faithfully present it in the story. Can there be any other truth to the old saw that great writers are sexless, raceless, and have no historical moment circumscribing their imagination and curiosity? So yes, to take up this meditation, "What is a character?" is to wonder, on the profoundest level, "What are the possibilities of being human, the parameters, the infinite, individual variations onto which our lives open?" Fiction, in a funny Buddhist sense, might even be called a Way.

You might object, as Gass proposed, that none of this scrupulous, fussy attention to detail forks up any "real" people. Mr. Cashmore is still made of words. Regardless, this method, this meditation, delivers devastatingly convincing phantoms—characters as convincing as Christopher Columbus, for what *do* we know of Columbus or of Crispus Attucks or of anyone who precedes us by a century or two, and therefore cannot be directly perceived? Surely we don't wish to limit knowing to direct perception only. History, journalism, biography involve, rightly or wrongly, a suspension of disbelief not unlike fiction's own. Columbus comes down to us partly through myth—meaning and concept—partly through narratives, partly through documents. And completely through language. It is the semblance of such historical detail, of this steady accumulation of specific (though for a novelist, fabricated) facts vividly bringing forth the biographical subject that each novelist—certainly John Gardner's sort of novelist—attempts quixotically to ape on his pages, creating the illusion of a life. With characters rendered in this spirit, plot usually takes care of itself, the progression of events often startling the writer, forcing him to scrap his outlines as a fictional "world" not his own (yet oddly his own), with its own laws and logic, emerges. Unfortunately, this has too seldom taken place in black fiction, and for reasons I've suggested earlier. Nor have black writers, on the whole, thematized the possibilities of fictional form for all that this sort of investigation might yield.

3

■ *Being and Form*

■ In the traditional, Asian martial arts, we say of a student after he has brilliantly executed a kata, or prearranged set of fighting moves, or done them *con brio,* that he has "honored the form." These forms predate the student in many cases by two or three centuries, have been executed over and over in Asia, America, and European countries, and by thousands of practitioners, old and young, Occidental and Oriental. Over the years they have evolved, of course, as different teachers have either updated or improved their movements, sometimes as many as a thousand moves in the more advanced forms. Each student is obliged to respect his predecessors, the spirit or meaning of each form, and, he one day realizes, he must interpret the ancient form in terms of the strengths and limitations of his own body (most Americans are not *built* like Asians), his particular time and place in order that the form may grow. Cross-cultural fertilization keeps the form alive. Saves it from senility. And death. Which is why many Asian teachers, refusing to instruct Yankees for centuries, finally gave in and opened the doors of the dojo and the kwoon.

During rare moments, the student will lose himself in the form. This occurs when he has repeated it hundreds of times, so that each movement is "programmed" into his body; he need not think consciously about the moves (in a real street fight, which only lasts about five seconds, there isn't time to think about which move to use). And for the advanced student, it sometimes feels as if the form performs *him.* If Ernest Hemingway could find playful analogues between writing and Western pugilism (and Yukio Mishima between writing and the samurai life of *bunburyodo*), then it's fair to compare the severe discipline of the Asian martial arts to writing, emphasizing (1) the galaxy of forms we inherit; (2) the need of every apprentice to master forms through relentless practice, study, and repetition; and (3) the duty incumbent on every apprentice to cultivate an attitude of "honoring the form," which is his inheritance as a Taekwondo or Wing Chun or Choy Li Fut stylist, moving the form forward through his own interpretation of possibilities made real by this historical moment.

Does this sound fanciful? Maybe it will seem less so when we consider that all literary forms are historical, evolving, and that on close analysis they reveal both the brilliance of our predecessors and their inevitable oversights and omissions—the limits of their understanding. Yet for all that, the vast number of fictional forms we inherit remain fertile fields for new explorations into meaning. No literary form is neutral. None is a value-empty vehicle into which we can simply "pour" the content of experience. Here, the ancient form-content notion proves itself false. Each form, whether it be a fairy tale or a non-narrative work, reveals a *Lebenswelt,* or vision of the world that is appropriate to its particular universe, and the use of any form will transfigure with startling results the "content" one wishes to express through it. And so in *The Will to Power,* in aphorism 818, Nietzsche can write, "A man is an artist to the extent to which he regards everything that inartistic people call 'form' as the actual substance, as the 'principal' thing." As a playful phenomenological variation, try this: tell *Native Son* in the voice of the storyteller in my own novel *Faith and the Good Thing;* or render Toomer's *Cane* with the gritty "realism" of the Wright school. Some things simply cannot be said or shown through the tradition of "realism" as we inherit it. Similarly, the forms that make up the ancestral roots of the modern story (yarns, tales, parables) must be transfigured considerably to employ, say, a twentieth-century existential sensibility, which Kafka, Borges, and Calvino have done with the parable.

In 1962 John Gardner and Lennis Dunlap published *The Forms of Fiction,* an anthology long out of print now.[1] One glimpses in his introductory essay on form in this work the seeds of Gardner's later thought on morality and technique in writing, seeds come fully into flower in *On Moral Fiction* (1978) and in his posthumously published handbook, *The Art of Fiction* (1983). In the latter, he argues that novice writers would do well to immerse themselves in a form or genre of popular fiction they love and intuitively know from repeated exposure, then compose a new work satisfying this form, following its conventions, and ambitiously play variations upon them; and here he also suggests that much great fiction exploits the possibilities of "genre crossing," or a cross-fertilization of one story form by another (or several). These works also uncover to a degree Gardner's own fictional conceits, for almost every novel he wrote used a different form—architectonic (*Sunlight Dialogues,* 1972), ghost-story-cum-college novel (*Mickelsson's Ghosts,* 1982), pastoral (*Nickle Mountain,* 1973), epic (*Jason and Medeia,* 1973), and more inventive forms such as his novel-within-a-novel (*October Light,* 1976, which received the National Book Critics Circle Award).

In *The Forms of Fiction,* Gardner, who like many other novelists learned only a smidgen of phenomenology but slipped into its spirit by instinct, descriptively analyzes several ancient forms modern writers rely heavily on. Gardner ranks the forms on what he perceives to be an ascending scale of internal complexity. He begins with the Sketch, the most primitive literary form, one basically used to create atmosphere and texture, often to nail down *haecceitas,* or "thisness," the specifics of an event, person, or landscape in all their individuality and fleeting beauty. It collects through meticulous detail and careful, loving observation the data of the world around us so that such information may be preserved. Every story, in one way or another, incorporates one or more Sketches of a person, place, or thing. But the Sketch itself, as a distinct form, seldom involves anything like plot and sometimes presents only the minimal requirements for Forster's definition of a story. Somewhat more complex is the Fable, or totem story, one of the oldest forms of storytelling known, indigenous to all cultures, identifiable in Asia with, say, the Buddhist Jātaka tales, and in the West with the epigrammatic, teaching stories of Aesop. Description is kept to a bare minimum. Everything is concrete, telegraphic, shown through specific action. A "moral" may or may not be appended to the end. It is a cousin of sorts to the Parable, beautiful examples of which occur in the New Testament stories supposedly told by Jesus (the story of the talents). In either its comic or its tragic variations, the Parable invokes a universe considerably more mysterious than that of the Fable. Underpinning its world are esoteric and moral laws often unknown to the protagonist, who must act nevertheless and, in ignorance of the way things work beneath the level of mere appearances, finds his actions turn out wrong or prove themselves too ambiguous for reason, so limited, to fully grasp, as in my story "The Education of Mingo." Often, we speak today of the Fable and the Parable in a single breath since both forms belong to the oral tradition and are "moral tales" of instruction. Yet even more distinct is the Yarn, a story produced by loggers, miners, fishermen, and the like—around campfires, one imagines, or places where men have come to work and, during the night, entertain each other with whopping lies about Paul Bunyan, High John the Conqueror, John Henry, and Stagolee. They are deliberately *not* to be believed. The intention of the narrator of the Yarn is to tell outrageous stories that stretch and shatter credibility, overblown accounts about characters expressed in superlatives: the *greatest* liar is the hero of the yarn, or the *strongest* woodsman, or the most *cunning* gambler. We listen incredulously, not believing a single word, our delight based on skepticism and wondering whether the storyteller can top the last, preposterous episode he's spun—by definition, the traditional Yarn is always episodic in structure, one outrageous lie after another. It shares this piecemeal quality with many folk and fairy tales, which are yet another step up in complexity. Tales provide the foundation for other forms such as the Apologue, generally display a design based on structural repetition (three tasks, for example, the hero or heroine must complete, each more difficult than the last), and, as scholars such as Bruno Bettelheim have shown, involve a completely rendered universe, one where a precisely detailed Sketch of a magic shield or sword coexists with a landscape only broadly described, some region we shall never be able to visit (an island, George Lucas's "galaxy far, far away") and where causation is often based more on poetic logic than on naturalism. The dead *must* rise, we notice in the Tale, because justice is unquestioned in this form and demands that a murdered person seek revenge on his killer, even beyond the grave. And so the dead walk. Angels intercede in human affairs. The logic of the heart holds the Tale together, fusing realism and fantasy in often profound gifts of the imagination.

The upshot of Gardner's discussion is just this: The modern short story or novel may assume the form of any of the above or, if you push this a bit further, any other narrative form people have employed—diaries, slave narratives, hymns, sermons, interlocking business documents—to clarify their experience. As Ishmael Reed once said, a novel can be the six o'clock news. Julius Lester's lovely *Black Folktales* (1969) indicates in the stories Lester retells that all these ancient forms prefigure contemporary black fiction. I would like to suggest that a modern short story lacking this dimension or level of formal invention is, like a story lacking a strong narrative voice, crippled or detotalized from the very first sentence. Its artistic possibilities are circumscribed. Without consciousness of this element, a writer has blinked a dimension of meaning, lost or ignored it, and disastrously so in ninety percent of the fiction published today, which has a depressing sameness, a formal one-dimensionality. Does this sound too severe? Can't we just tell stories without worrying about the forms or traditions from which they spring? In *The Educated Imagination,* our finest myth critic, Northrup Frye, tells us otherwise:

> Every form of literature has a pedigree, and we can trace its descent back to the earliest times. A writer's desire to write can only come from previous experience of literature, and he'll start by imitating whatever he's read, which usually means what people around him are writing. This provides for him what is called a convention, a certain typical and socially accepted way of writing.... After working in this convention for a while, his own distinctive sense of form will develop out of his knowledge of literary technique. He doesn't create out of nothing; and whatever he has to say he can say only in a recognizably literary way.[2]

Frye's charming little book, and his entire theory of literature, reminds us that "literature can derive its forms only from itself: they can't exist outside literature, any more than musical forms like the sonata and the fugue can exist outside music." And he reminds us, too, how story plots in the air around us are as old as humanity itself. Correction: *are* humanity itself. The story of Bluebeard rings behind every contemporary thriller; pastoral conventions, behind westerns. Recycled primitive folktales can be glimpsed in the fiction of William Faulkner, or Tennessee Williams, or Toni Morrison; and Christian and classical myths, beneath more stories than anyone can name. "Everything is new," says Frye, "and yet recognizably the same kind of thing as the old." Or at least it is for writers with "educated" imaginations, who find in the finest work of their predecessors models—artistic and metaphysical—for the future. To paraphrase Kant, imagination without education is blind; education without imagination, empty. Ideally, the two coalesce in great fiction—as in science—to solve objective artistic problems handed down by our predecessors, black and white, who provided us a path to walk on but who could not themselves finish the journey. Nor shall we, since the efflorescence of meaning is endless. And so, though they grumble, my graduate students are all required to write carefully detailed outlines in a variety of forms. More, even, they must research a form not used for a major work in the last hundred years—some literary dinosaur once popular in the West or the East, then pushed aside by the course of fiction's evolution—and then carefully plot a new story using its conventions. Nothing they wish to say about their Aunt Ethel or personal feelings is sacrificed. On the contrary, knowledge of form "informs," guides their feelings. As Frye puts it, "To bring anything really to life in literature we can't be lifelike: we have to be literature-like."

If this thesis is workable, it's obvious that black fiction could benefit greatly from the revitalizing influences of cross-cultural fertilization (already present in our lives, indeed as the very stuff of our lives) found in formal variations and technical virtuosity. It would be a pleasure, I believe, to see our writers experimenting with prerealistic forms of the seventeenth century as Russell Banks, one of our most prolific writers, did in *The Relation of My Imprisonment* (1982) (we were in America then, too), with the *fabliau,* the classic sea story, the utopian novel, and a galaxy of other forms that are our inheritance as writers. This inheritance cannot be emphasized enough. First, because we, as artists, work in an ever-expanding community. And second, because this curious, social, intersubjective side of art is, as the best estheticians report, central to the artistic personality and the creative process.

"Every young man's heart," Malraux says in *The Voices of Silence,* "is a graveyard in which are inscribed the names of a thousand dead artists, but whose only actual denizens are a few mighty, often antagonistic ghosts." This startling, spectral image points to a fact that every black writer is all too painfully aware of, that the young artist is haunted by greatness, the mighty presence of a Wright, an Ellison, a Du Bois. That he "has not to make a choice between his personal 'vision' and his master or masters, but between certain canvases and certain other canvases," to which he as a young (or old) hopeful master must *respond.* "The poet," Malraux says, "is haunted by a voice with which his words must harmonize . . . a poor poet would he be who never heard that inner voice; a poor novelist for whom the novel was no more than a tale!" This *more* for Malraux is the vision of Being contained in the forms of expression our forebears have imposed upon experience, one that quickens the imagination of the apprentice and demands—if he or she is to one day achieve greatness—an original reply. But on *what* is originality founded? Malraux writes:

> Even a Rembrandt, a Piero della Francesca, or a Michelangelo is not, at the dawn of his career, a man who sees more vividly than others the infinite diversity of things; he is a youth enraptured by certain paintings which he carries with him to divert his gaze from the world of appearances.

So it is with innovative film directors, who long for the opportunity to re-create or to improve on a brilliant scene or camera shot, to honor it in their own work by going it one better. And so it is with young writers who have been seduced by the realm of art, a universe that is, one must confess, separate from everyday experience. Often they begin, as Gardner suggests, with shameless imitation, itself a form of love and reverence. But creators always move beyond the pastiche, "advancing from one world of forms," as Malraux says, "to another world of forms . . . from one world of words to another," oftentimes melding elements of several artists who may contradict each other, though each is admired for a unique contribution, until they have achieved mastery of the forms that precede their lives, their times; and into this tradition of literature, this ongoing groping for sense, they project a new vision and invent the fictional vehicles to embody it.

Perhaps, then, it is for this reason that we demand formal virtuosity from our greatest writers, the journeyman's proof that they can write *anything* because "every great style of the past impresses us as being a special interpretation of the world" or, one might say, because each style simultaneously opens and closes off possibilities for interpretation and exploration, thereby necessitating, for an endlessly curious artist, a facility with many approaches. For Malraux, "every style, in fact, creates its own universe by selecting and incorporating such elements of reality as enable the artist to focus all the shape of things on some essential part of man." Time and again, men and women have written masterpieces with only a small bag of tricks (D. H. Lawrence, Flannery O'Connor, Richard Wright), and who wishes to criticize an artist who does only one thing well? Still, our greatest respect must be reserved for the protean writer, the performer like Chaucer or Shakespeare, who slides from genre to genre, style to style, leaving his or her distinctive signature on each form lovingly transfigured and pushed toward new possibilities. No creator, black or white, can be exempt from this standard. No genuine artist would wish to be.

■ Black Writers since 1970

4

■ *The Men*

■ Our most interesting writers are often those who consciously formulate for themselves an esthetic, a project, or ensemble of artistic and cultural problems common to us all that they hope to address, then provisionally to answer in their work. In the fiction of these writers who, I admit, are rare, we see the same fundamental questions raised year in, year out, approached or attacked from different creative angles, and with different literary tools as they wrestle from book to book to embody more perfectly a vision, or to repair artistic oversights of the past. Such a project requires, in some cases, that they transform or personalize the expressive instrument—language—to suit their purposes, and sometimes completely reenvision the enterprise of fiction by breaking with convention, challenging current literary practice by reaching back to an earlier age of master artists or by forging entirely new techniques. This is doubtlessly the work of a lifetime, a long one. Often their work is unfinished at their deaths, but this standard of striving is the litmus test we must use to separate the serious artists from the hacks, the commercial drones, the well-meaning fakers who blunder along blindly from one book to the next with no grander esthetic guide than the Bestseller List or the latest literary fashions. For lack of a better word, these artists who are reaching for new ground are often called "experimental" (an umbrella term too vague to mean much of anything) by reviewers too confused, or lazy, to take a hard look at what the writers are doing. Obviously, their originality, or the eccentricity of their esthetic may, in a few cases, lead as often to failure—sometimes a grand, noble failure that inspires and intrigues those who follow—as it does to success. But generally we all benefit from their pioneering, lonely ventures into the realms of the possible, and such artists deserve our gratitude and respect.

One such writer is Clarence Major. For twenty years Major and his colleagues in the Fiction Collective, a cooperative publishing venture started in the early 1970s by a handful of "experimental" writers (among them Ronald Sukenick, Jonathan Baumbach, and Raymond Federman), have been on the cutting edge of nontraditional fiction in America. Personally, I am seldom at ease with the results of this sort of writing, which provides more intellectual than dramatic pleasure, but I am appreciative of Major's steady, unyielding effort to interpret for black American writing the European style of esthetic thought that begins probably with Laurence Sterne's *Tristram Shandy,* threads through James Joyce, Gertrude Stein, and Samuel Beckett, and crops up more or less in the work of William Gass, John Barth, Robert Coover, and John Hawkes. Major has combined his many talents as a much-anthologized poet, painter, teacher, international lecturer, lexicographer (he is the author of the very useful *Dictionary of Afro-American Slang,* 1970), editor, and novelist in such highly original books as *Reflex and Bone Structure* (1975), *No* (1973), and the multimedia *Emergency Exit* (1979), to which I shall devote this discussion, for it is in this unusual, often rewarding work that Major reveals the radical, uncompromising character of his approach to art.

Emergency Exit is about, among other things, the failure of fiction. The "death" of the novel. And the black writer's loss of faith in traditional realism and all that that implies: Christianity, bourgeois culture, and conventional morality. It is a text for the twentieth-century breakdown of belief in language, consciousness, even love, a kind of unflinching meditation on the Abyss as well as a perfect illustration of Raymond Federman's "Four Propositions" in *Surfiction: Fiction Now and Tomorrow,* a handbook on alternative writing. In these propositions, which form a Surfictionist manifesto, we find a very different attitude toward the writer's relationship to his reader: "The writer will no longer be considered a prophet, a philosopher, or even a sociologist who predicts, teaches or reveals absolute truths, nor will he be looked upon (admiringly and romantically) as the omnipresent, omniscient, and omnipotent creator, but he will stand on equal footing with the reader in their efforts to make sense of the language common to both of them."[1] And there is in Surfiction a different view of characters: "The people of fiction . . . will also no longer be well-made characters who carry with them a fixed meaning. . . . Their being will be more genuine, more true-to-life in fact, because they will not appear to be simply what they are; they will be what they are: word beings." Federman continues to outline this new style of literary practice as one that will make the reader an active participant in fashioning the work's meaning that in traditional art he has "simply received, passively." This is, according to Federman, an approach that will alter the very arrangement of words on the page, disrupt linear time in the reading experience, as in Federman's novel *Take It or Leave It* (1976), and basically trash the bourgeois presuppositions of fiction.

The more you ponder this kind of writing, the more clearly do you see that Federman (in theory) and Major (in practice) are asking you, as a reader, to *work* to find sense in their stories. Asking this of Americans may be dangerous indeed. On the downside, the doubt these writers have in the power of fiction traditionally conceived compels them to mock self-consciously the process of writing itself, to short-circuit "drama" before it starts, and, like nervous magicians, to explain their tricks as they perform them. The effect is like that of lifting a curtain on the gimmicks and gears grinding behind the novel. And what is wrong with that in small doses? It's a testament to the writer's and the reader's own sense of play, their refusal to take this work or the world too seriously. Ironically, though, this serendipity seems at war with the grim, unhappy vision of Being that surfaces so often in Surfiction. Beneath all the linguistic gamesmanship, just below the surface, the experiences Federman's writer and reader have created are displacement, nihilism, and disintegration. On the positive side, this demand by the Surfictionists such as Major that the readers stay alert from paragraph to paragraph, and question from one line to the next the very enterprise of writing and reading, is an appeal to our intellectual integrity and freedom. And his promise to keep us off balance for our own good makes interesting demands on Major himself: namely, he places upon himself the yoke of relentlessly being inventive, never flagging in imagination, never turning in the same performance twice.

In *Emergency Exit,* Major's aim is to present "flashes of people—not *real* people . . . responding to a complex situation where a certain motif is persistent." That motif, what Major calls the book's "central metaphor," is the mysterious, feminine power of *doorways* and *thresholds*. "The doorway of life," as the structuring metaphor in *Emergency Exit,* is, once we go beyond the doorway as cliché, a tiered image so primordial, so mythic it embodies the "ritual of the in-and-out motion of things, negative and positive, life and death, rhythm and the static, the inlet and the exit, the male and the female, being and not being." Philosophically,

Major's book promises to explore the lived impact of these polarities that run the length of Western intellectual history, dichotomies exacerbated in modern times by Descartes's bifurcation of man in *The Meditations,* but much older, dialectical by nature, and haloed in mystery. Major situates this interesting theme of *openings* and *closures* in Inlet, Connecticut, a place of "purity, cleanliness, and proper conduct," and in the tangled love affairs of four people "trying to get to the Place before the Door closes."

Allen Morris, a "mentally black" Harlem drug peddler, very dark, visits the Inlet home of his fashionably Pan-Africanist lover, Julie Ingram, during the absence of her parents. His visit, which provides the novel's story line, emphasizes the breakdown of communication in Inlet. The Ingram family and Al have nothing in common, except Julie. "It drives me insane," rages Al, "to go downtown to see how the white world is." Privileged, but insecure in her blackness, Julie is at pains to understand Al and to love her father, "a bigtime civil rights guy" who "opened the door for many colored people." Where Al grew up restless, "like a character in a Richard Wright story," and realized in reform school "that the world was a shithole and most of the people in it are shitheads," Julie traveled in East Africa when her father worked for the American Information Service. She is "colored but not like any colored persons I've known," thinks Al. "Heard about them. Saw them at a distance. What's she see in me."

Even as he develops this relationship—a serious conflict of black economic and class differences—Major reminds us to keep our distance, invites us to "watch them eat their words, I mean bacon and eggs," in intentional disruptions of drama that recall Gass's characters in his story "Willie Master's Lonesome Wife" (1968), who repeatedly remind us, "I'm only a string of noises, after all," "These words are all I am. Believe me. Pity me"; and in the work's last line Gass sums everything up by saying, "You have fallen into art—return to life." For many Surfictionists, we are childlishly naive to empathize or feel for people who are, ontologically, made of printer's ink. There is some fun in this kind of authorial play, but it's mainly when Major backs off from postmodernism and lets his characters act according to the natures he's given them that Al and Julie struggle "to blunt the equipment of stammering," and thereby achieve a dignity, a presence in the novel second only to that of her father, Jim.

Of all the characters in *Emergency Exit,* Jim Ingram most deeply suffers the experience of dualism and the strangeness of doorways. "Linear in his outlook," perhaps even "an old stuffed shirt," he fears and worships the sacred blood-fertility-birth dimension of his wife, Deborah, and Julie—fears, you might even say, the presence of a powerful level of ritual and meaning in their lives as women and a promise of transcendence beyond dualism. Major defines the threshold as the reconciliation of the sacred and the profane, for the "door" is, from time out of mind, a feminine symbol that "contains all the implications of the symbolic hole," or exit. Put another way, Jim Ingram experiences vaginal cavities as a gateway to grace, an idea also found in Major's first novel, *All Night Visitors* (1969). This is the primitive vision of woman as the vehicle of Being, birth, regeneration, a vision that will horrify feminists, I know, falling as it does into a mystifying of women, but Major does much to correct this in his most recent, award-winning novel, *My Amputations* (1986), and in *Such Was the Season* (1987), a beautiful tale told from an elderly black woman's point of view. Although Jim dismisses Al as a "thug from Harlem," both men long for redemption, to be integrated, "naked and trembling in the doorway, exposed to everything," because once there, on the threshold, "inside and outside pressures are . . . equalized."

Yet redemption escapes Jim Ingram· Roslyn, his white secretary, seduces him—according to Julie—to win a bet that even staid Jim Ingram can be laid. Prepared now to divorce Deborah for Roslyn, afraid of Julie, feeling "life is so fucking sad so goddamn sad every way you look," Jim, with his dilemma, holds our interest, but as before, Major steps in at the moment of greatest dramatic intensity, reminding us that he is "just playing a game of fiction." Some readers, I fear, will find this maddening, though Major is only being true to his intention of pushing the reflexive turn of contemporary fiction to its limits. He provides a list of twenty names for his book and hopes we'll choose one. The best are "Course on Writing" and "Realism: A Dark Light," because his real concern in *Emergency Exit* is with a sustained destruction of traditional realism. "A scholar once asked me," writes Major in the novel, "are you trying to write like Barth you know Barth in his stories always sounds like he's teaching a creative writing class I don't like that kind of stuff I think it's misdirected it's just a gimmick."

Despite the deliberate jettisoning of dramatic possibilities in *Emergency Exit,* some of Major's other devices work rather well. He includes two wonderfully comic, brilliant sketches that capture his subjects—

one called "The African," another, "The Black Professor." Because "this situation we're in is being rendered in terms of images and dramatic description," he effectively exploits the technique of brief, photorealist perceptions of Inlet that echo the absurdist humor of Beat poet Bob Kaufman in "Heavy Water Blues." The effect is, largely, that of abstract impressionism:

> The woman washed her back with a brush. The spam grew from the table filling the apartment and when it reached the bathroom where she was washing her back it consumed her and clogged the water pipes. She never even made it to the door.

Emphasizing the sleight-of-hand possibilities of fiction, and the fact that any *document* from the everyday world can be used, as well as the strategy of such pop artists as Andy Warhol to isolate ordinary objects in the art gallery and thereby make them interesting, Major gives us half a dozen nonfictional texts to create the novel's setting: a page of names from the Inlet telephone directory; two pages that catalogue books from the Inlet Public Library; definitions from a score of dictionaries—ancient and modern—that define his metaphors (the approach here is Melvillian, where, in the preface to *Moby Dick,* we receive so many definitions of the whale, so many profiles of meaning from so many various perspectives, that it resonates, hazy, with a surplus of meaning); portions of letters he's received; and quotations from fellow Fiction Collective authors and friends like Federman, who writes, "All great fiction, to a large extent, is a reflection on itself, on its own proliferating mechanisms, rather than reality."

Trapped in this "proliferating mechanism," Al and Julie watch their love affair disintegrate, broken finally by Julie's refusal to believe that a white man fired a shot at Al. "You can't believe it because you're too white yourself," he shouts. "And the minute he said it he knew it was the beginning of their separation." Love is the subject of another of Major's lists. Quoting twenty-two authors, he advances the idea that love is "a power too strong to be overcome by anything but flight" (Cervantes); "a mutual misunderstanding" (Oscar Wilde); or an experience that "in itself, in the form of longing and deprivation, lowers the self-regard" (Sigmund Freud). What Major calls the problem of the "self searching for the fullness of self" through the mystical body of woman is, plainly, an impossible quest. Al sleeps with Julie's mother, Deborah, even "carries her across the threshold" before he loses Julie, and Jim, feeling miserable, stays in his holding pattern with Roslyn. And what of the author, who is clearly as much a "character" in *Emergency Exit* as the others?

As the novel ends, Major focuses on the author himself. "In a small house in the countryside the author was dying at an early age then he recovered and nobody knew why or how." He tells his wife, who ironically calls him "Drama," that "I want to go out across that threshold into the sunlight." Half-naked, barefoot, he lumbers outside as "a few hundred characters from this very novel stood around." Major puns, "Drama was taking command! He was coming out." Continuing, he crawls into the sunlight:

> The minute he reached the warm light of the sun he began to burn. First the right arm then his face and left arm. Also the part of his chest not covered by the nightgown. Little flames began to leap from his face and arms. But he did not stop.

No one can doubt that the real hero of *Emergency Exit* is Clarence Major. When fiction's power to ensorcel is thrown into doubt, we are left with the author alone in the center ring, creating his fabulations not from life observed (the objective world has collapsed into the self, which itself is in doubt) but from the materials of his own imagination, his notebooks, letters, and lectures on the dilemma of the novelist in the late twentieth century. Other writers probe these same affairs. But among black writers, Major has the territory covered. Almost single-handedly, he has applied himself to exploring the sobering critique of Alain Robbe-Grillet, even expanding on this to interface it with the investigations of such surrealists as André Breton and Raymond Roussell and the Dadaists, creating fiction that, as critic Arthur P. Davis says in his article "Novels of the New Black Renaissance" (1978), "make the experimental fiction of Ishmael Reed seem like child's play." Of greater importance is that Major, like experimental filmmakers who opposed the formula movies from major studios in the 1930s, has pioneered strategies, techniques, and ways of thinking about black fiction that will, I believe, gain wider currency someday among more conventional writers interested in their creative options from one line to the next. Few, I'm guessing, will follow him fully into all the principles of Surfiction, but he leaves us a body of work that ensures his place among the innovative writers of the age.

One of Major's epigraphs in *Emergency Exit,* quoting Eric Dolphy,

"If you try to do something different in this country, people put you down for it," could easily have been used by Ishmael Reed for any of his novels. Like Major, this fascinating man has made a career of challenging white, Western forms imposed upon our experience; but unlike Major, Reed is obliged by his "Neo-Hoodoo" esthetic, as he calls it, to regard Surfiction and the models Major uses as just another way of buying into European epistemology. Among contemporary black writers, Reed is our fast-talking wildman, our esthetic terrorist and comedian, a barnstorming provacateur who deploys brutal satire to bait white liberals and blacks both, to lampoon politicians, and all by his lonesome to lock horns, not with feminists of the first intellectual caliber, whom he respects, but with the imitative, rank-and-file "Moonies," as he once described them to me over dinner. I'm talking about the man, a kind of latter-day George Schuyler and Wallace Thurman combined, with a little Swift thrown in, who in June 1986 went on the nationally broadcast television program "Tony Brown's Journal" and who earlier in March, on the day of the Academy Award nominations, had appeared on national television to remind viewers of the artistic and moral flaws in Alice Walker's *The Color Purple,* a work so sacred to many women readers that most black writers were too timid to criticize it in public. And, as if this weren't enough, Reed followed up with a novel I'd have been too chicken to write: *Reckless Eyeballing* (1986), which claims that white feminists and black women are in league to drive black male writers into oblivion. Whether his charge is true or not, this much is sure: Ishmael Reed is his own person. There is no one like him. He has courage. And he's smart. While many may damn certain aspects of his fiction, most are delighted by the very, outrageous *idea* of Ishmael Reed—his style of calling shots as he sees them—and feel grateful he's still out there, raising hell.

From the beginning of his career, Reed, equipped with one of Hemingway's "built-in shit detectors," has championed, as a book and magazine publisher, the work of nonwhite writers, Asian as well as black—for example, by publishing Shawn Wong's *Homebase* (1979); he has promoted nontraditionalists, white and black, male and female, and waged a one-man war against what he identifies as the oversights of the East Coast literary establishment (themes of hidden conspiracies against minorities and innovators run throughout his work from *Mumbo Jumbo* (1972) to *Reckless Eyeballing*). On what basis does he make this criticism?

In his introduction to *19 Necromancers from Now* (1970), Reed describes the "black experience" as being diverse. He says that each black writer is his own esthetician. Sixty percent of his essay is a criticism of liberal artistic attitudes toward black writing, prejudices that exalt European culture over all others and deny the authenticity of popular forms of fiction such as westerns, mysteries, and science fiction, and also the integrity of colloquial speech and ethnic slang. Reed goes on to say, perhaps in his own defense, that contemporary black writers break with Western forms, which he calls "diseased" because they are tied to Western metaphysics. In place of this, a "dark heathenism" is needed, a mixture of popular (folk) elements, individualism, and spirituality, with the supernatural reintroduced to our understanding of how the universe works. In *Interviews with Black Writers* (1973), he expands on these ideas, arguing that storytelling logically and historically precedes the novel as a form. In terms of his own art, Reed describes his characters as being cartoons, where the cartoon is seen as a caricature, a boiling down of a person to the essential elements; in his own words, his characters are intended to be like voodoo dolls constructed on the basis of generic qualities, dominant impressions, a single feeling perhaps. This delivers, he says, the character's *soul,* or, in terms of the art of caricature, the broad, essential strokes that make the character identifiable to everyone. Elaborate character description, delicate conjuring of setting and social gestures are, for Reed in this interview, boring and excessive material.

To a very great extent, Reed's ideas on art present a highly personalized twist on the Black Aesthetic and cultural nationalism. However, he adds a few new wrinkles. First, he is an antinovelist. Like the Surfictionists, his books are often *about* writing. Not about the breakdown of fiction, though. Instead, Reed's fiction and criticism feed on the accumulated history of black literature. The period of the late 1960s is probably the first time in history when a black writer could play humorous riffs on the works of his predecessors because until the 1920s, as we know, there simply wasn't that much black American fiction around to form a solid tradition that could be challenged or parodied. Nor does Reed fully agree with all the black nationalists. Like them, he rejects the idea of white liberals (he sees it as their idea) that black writing must be "universal," an idea he calls Atonist. Aton is the name taken by the evil Egyptian god, Osiris. It means "burner of growing things." For Reed, an Atonist can be on the political left or right as long as he agrees on the sacredness of Western culture. In his novel *Mumbo Jumbo,* the Atonists include Sigmund Freud, black Marxists, and anyone who believes in the Protestant work ethic, self-denial, Western high culture, Christianity, glumness of any sort, and tragedy. Counterpoised to this is Reed's "Hoodoo" esthetic, a new heathenism represented in *Mumbo Jumbo* by Papa Labas, an "astral-detective," who is "in harmony with all things," and who reappears in Reed's later work. Reed's esthetic is also represented by "Jes Grew," an antiplague that is carried by blacks and, in fact, is the Harlem Renaissance seen as a spiritual manifestation of black creativity taking the form of a psychic epidemic of artistic activity and dancing.

Close analysis reveals that, like Major, Reed expects his readers to sweat a bit to seize the overall meaning of his works. In place of familiar characterization and conventional plot, he substitutes an ever-changing montage of elements he has made distinctly his own: (1) actual history and popular trivia about blacks in the 1920s to critique American history and European culture in *Mumbo Jumbo,* and about slavery in *Flight to Canada* (1976), where slave owners drink the milk of bondswomen for breakfast; (2) a fairly complete reinterpretation of Western civilization by way of his affection for popular literature dismissed by the "Atonists," and by use of elements of Egyptian and vodun mythology to present an alternate vision of how people should live; and finally, true to his interest in folk forms of storytelling, (3) parodies of the plots of genre fiction—the western in *Yellowback Radio Broke Down* (1969), into which Reed inserts a hoodoo black cowboy, detective novels in *Mumbo Jumbo,* and the novel of popular history in *Flight to Canada.*

All in all, this is a remarkable mélange, one consistent pretty much throughout Reed's later novels, even with his personal style, which, as he says of American culture in general, is "eclectic." It is also interesting from the standpoint of deconstructionist criticism. No one has discussed this aspect of Reed's work more thoroughly than MacArthur Fellow and critic Henry Louis Gates, Jr., in his article "The 'Blackness of Blackness': A Critique of the Sign and the Signifying Monkey" (1983), and I urge readers to consider Reed's body of work in light of Gates's provocative analysis. If his fiction presents a problem to some readers, the reason is perhaps because what Reed, who is unique and individual, firebombs us with is a freewheeling criticism of the West, offbeat yet plausible facts drawn from his voluminous readings in the history of race relations and, regarding his strategy, the literary equivalent of a Warner Brothers cartoon. All these strategies are effective in the end, and entertain as well as enlighten a little, but do they come together in a single, unified vision of life? My feeling is that his work could not be otherwise than it is and remain true to his ideas. A more systematic approach, one using vivid characters, Aristotelian mimetic principles, and poetically charged language, would be for Reed "Atonist," or spoiled by Western philosophy's demand for a certain kind of coherence, completeness, and consistency in any expression. It would betray the rebellious spirit of his personal style, as well as wreck his satirical intent, for by taking a voodoo doll from the level of caricature to that of a character with the illusion of depth and three-dimensionality would surely make it impossible for Reed and his fans, of which I'm one, to laugh at them or see them in one dimension only. We would, in other words, begin to empathize and feel their pain. The first note of tragedy would ring. And all satirical possibility would end.

Reed's persistence in arguing that we appreciate the diversity in serious black writing is borne out, obviously in his work and in that of Major, and also in the imaginative fiction of Samuel Delany. If memorable, enduring fiction has any distinguishing quality, it is simply this: imaginative storytelling reinforced by massive technique. And for a long time now some have claimed that the last stronghold of imaginative American literature is science fiction, its proponents pointing to such masters as Ursula Le Guin and Stanislaw Lem and tracing its origins back to Plato's *Republic*. Whether this is so is debatable, but one thing that no one can deny is that Delany has made a lasting contribution to the "New Wave" or "social" fringe of science fiction, though he doesn't call it that, as a novelist and literary critic. And, among black writers, he stands pretty much alone, except for a few talented newcomers, as the first author to explore systematically the possibilities of a tradition created in the modern era by Mary Shelley and Jules Verne, then nailed down with definition by H. G. Wells. We remember George Schuyler's playful *Black No More* as an early science-fiction effort by a black writer, but it is Delany, a multiple-winner of the Nebula Award, who published his first novel at age nineteen, who "goes the distance" in addressing dilemmas specific to the twentieth century, as, for example, in his best-known novel, *Babel-17* (1966), a work that applies linguistics to questions of identity and our experience of reality. In addition to being intellectually ambitious, his growing body of work exhibits a formal range that is rare in black fiction and, in such works as *Flight from Nevèryön* (1985), a prose style that leaps and pirouettes, conjures imaginative worlds as vivid as any outside your window, with sentences that are fluid and fully voiced and, by virtue of such beauty—such attention to music and the mutability of language—satisfy every esthetic standard. Consider this 100-plus-word sentence from *Flight from Nevèryön:*

> No doubt in the palace his rough, if scarred, good looks would cause (he dreamed) a few noble ladies to catch their breath; and perhaps even once, at some great party, into which he'd wandered only by accident, he'd exchange a few lines of banter with the Child Empress herself, whose reign is glittering and glorious, causing waves of jealousy and ire among the lords gathered at the affair, so that, after a month or so of such dalliance, his patroness (who by this time, would hopefully have taken up another lover, perhaps a young nobleman whose arrogant ways would make her fondly recall her nights and noons with him) would finally secure him an officer's commission in the Imperial Army, at some fascinating outpost in some exotic mountain hold, sending him on to who-knows-what great and gainful adventures. . . .

Shrewdly, this sentence appears at the opening of a section (or chapter), plunging us immediately into the fictional dream, entrapping us by its length since every period is, after all, a reprieve or rest for the reader, one Delany does not permit. A blend of "periodic" constructions (where the sense is not completed until the end of the line) and ones that are "loose" (where qualifying clauses are tacked onto the end of the principal clauses), this sentence generates through its movement a kind of suspense, a rising and falling motion; yet at the same time it is characterized by lightness and grace, the feel one gets from relaxed, unhurried conversation. It is the perfect model for the sentence as described by J. H. Fowler in *Essay Writing* (1899): "The cadence as well as the sense of a sentence should rise gradually toward the middle, should, if necessary, continue there on a level for a brief period, and should then descend in a gradation corresponding to its ascent." Never mind whether such elegance is a product of instinct or education, native talent or sweat; the point remains the same: Delany is, without qualification, a "writer's writer" who entertains as he educates his readers, and is someone who provides a model of genuine excellence for future black fiction.

As does William Melvin Kelley, a novelist of great technical skill, as he demonstrates in his faintly Joycean novel, *Dunsford's Travels Everywhere* (1970), influenced in parts by the word punning, neologisms, and forcing of language to its limits in *Finnegans Wake*. And in such earlier novels as *A Different Drummer* (1962), which explores the impact on a white community when its black residents all move away, inspired by a Moses-like figure named Tucker Caliban; and in *dem* (1967), an at times brutally effective satire of race relations premised on a quirk of genetics—a white, middle-class woman bears twins, one white (from her husband) and one black (from her maid's boyfriend). Many critics, Addison Gayle among them, and Arthur P. Davis, find Kelley's involvement with the Black Arts Movement a crucial dimension in his fiction, and while I think this is so, I also suspect that readers will be more delighted by Kelley's imagination than by his political leanings. He is a natural, a gifted, and a controlled storyteller. A good example of Kelley's skill can be found in his wickedly comic 1968 short story, "The Dentist's Wife," a modern *fabliau* set in Harlem. A dentist, very bourgeois, wants badly to divorce his wife, Robena, so that he can marry his beautiful assistant, Jean, and offers a black hustler named Carlyle Bedlow a thousand dollars if he'll seduce his wife and get snapshots the dentist can use in court. Like the short fiction of Chesnutt, this story *as* a story is as structurally tight as any artist could wish. With the "substructure" of plot in place, Kelley is able, quite masterfully, to let the story's "superstructure" (sociological facts for texture, his generous sense of humor, and crisp dialogue) reel out to provide the kinds of rewards only good storytelling can deliver. He is, in all these works, a technician both apprentice and journeyman writers can admire.

Another writer strong in comic yet serious entertainment is Al Young, a veteran poet, novelist, free-lance journalist, musician, and screenwriter. He is distinguished by the emphasis in his large body of work on a gentle vision of black American life that is, at bottom, harmonious and spiritual. Young is a philosophically interesting writer, as readers will come to see in his forthcoming novel, *Seduction by Light;* he has, like Toomer, exposed himself to the universe of Eastern metaphysics, specifically to the meditation methods of Yogananda and the large, distinguished body of work by Eknath Easwaran, who is, in my opinion, our most trustworthy interpreter of Oriental thought. In short, nothing of importance in the universe of global culture and consciousness is lost on Al Young. As poet Richard Shelton described him in his introduction of Young at a 1986 meeting for the Associated Writing Programs, he is beyond all doubt a "man of letters." In contrast to the Angry School of black writing in the 1960s, which Young has criticized in his poem "A Dance for Militant Dilettantes," he provides a refreshing difference. His heart, if this doesn't sound corny to say, is with the "common folk," as was Langston Hughes's, with black people whose lives display endurance, folk wisdom, and the sort of humor Sterling Brown might appreciate. In his novels such as *Snakes* (1970), chronicling the life of a young musician, and *Sitting Pretty* (1976), a comic and vivid character sketch of an aging black man who becomes a radio talk show celebrity, Young shows just how well he can handle authentic black dialect that nails down the music of rural and urban black voices, and also demonstrates a talent for stories that sometimes disarm a reader with their substitution of quiet insights and maturity for the bristling rage of the Black Nationalists. In his "Statement on Aesthetics, Poetics, Kinetics" in *New Black Voices* (1972), he expresses himself as a writer primarily concerned with the communal spirit underlying artistic activity, which he sees as a moral, humanizing activity, especially today in a postindustrial society where individuals are so easily lost in the crowd, an activity that comes down hard on the idea of black life (all life) as a process. In his work the individual is in movement, a process of continual change; "dancing" seems to be his favorite metaphor, so that no one is trapped in a situation, good or bad, for very long. In other words, Young emphasizes hope but adds that to complete his or her *telos* each individual must surrender completely to feeling and faith. Like that of many writers to emerge from the 1960s, his interest in black music (*Bodies and Souls* [1981], *Snakes*) stems from a belief that music, as a creative act, expresses not only feeling and becoming but community as well.

No question that we've seen this before in the Black Arts Movement. But in Young's novels, at the heart of his fictional process, there is no hatred. Only a weariness with the more extreme political postures of the late 1960s and early 1970s. There is also a wisdom that comes with age, from having observed a great deal of human behavior, which leads to both faint disenchantment and great compassion, and from these emerges a noble yet slightly nervous belief that there is, and perhaps always has been, a basic harmony to Being that cannot be broken. An author must *will* himself, I suspect, to write as Young does; he must will positive, time-honored values, as he conceives them—faith, love, a belief in family life—against the staggering evidence at his elbow for despair and disintegration, his intention being to balance the darker moments so easy to dramatize with other experiences that soften the terror, the pain of dislocation, the horrors of black history, and to leave us in the end—as in many of Young's books and better poems—with a feeling of thanksgiving, which is damned hard to dramatize. It is *easy*, as one of my students puts it, to be "despairingly effective" in fiction. And nearly impossible to deliver convincingly a portrait of black life that is, to use one of John Gardner's phrases, "life-affirmative." Al Young tries. And in *Sitting Pretty*—a crowd pleaser when he reads it aloud to large audiences—he succeeds in delivering characters whose humanity transcends stereotypes. In this fact alone, Young provides a necessary transition from the hysterical, race-baiting black fiction of an earlier decade.

Also important as transition figures from the 1960s are John Mc Cluskey, Jr., Leon Forrest, and John Edgar Wideman, who, like Young, display in their work a powerful love for "everyday" black people, our elders, the people for whom no biographies shall ever be written, but whose lives reveal models of heroism and love. The very logic of their fiction, the *reason* they write, a reader soon realizes, is to mine their memories for portraits of black people who have made an impression on them, then to preserve such remembrance on the page. Critic Elizabeth A. Schultz has written persuasively in her article "The Heirs of Ralph Ellison" (1978) that McCluskey's wandering musician, Mack, in *Look What They Done to My Song* (1974) begins where Ellison's hero ends, listening to the blues. But in Mack's case he is on a beach, playing his saxophone, then embarks upon a beautifully lyric journey that takes him deeper and deeper into the lives of a wide diversity of black people—derelicts, radicals, a gay actor, and religious folks—and more importantly to the realization that "I am black, and human and must not deny my heart. In tune, certainly, with the rhythms reserved for me."

In his second novel, *Mr. America's Last Season Blues* (1982), Mc-Cluskey widens his range of black portraits and significantly deepens each in lovingly evoked detail, structuring this story around the spiritual crisis of an ex-football player with an ensemble of troubles: a "lost" brother pursuing their father's killer, a marriage disintegrating, a lover's son railroaded by an unjust court after a white boy is killed, and his protagonist's effort to regain a bit of his gridiron glory. In characterization, this second novel is an advance over McCluskey's first, but his talent is most evident in some of his shorter fiction, especially "Chicago Jubilee Rag," which was cited among the outstanding stories of 1983 by the Pushcart Prize jurors. There, he applies his imagination to history, bringing together an elderly Frederick Douglass, an artistically insecure Paul Lawrence Dunbar, and Scott Joplin in Chicago at a Colored American Day fair. Just as this story demonstrates McCluskey's ability to breathe life into historically accurate fiction that *opens* the past in such a way that we feel the emotions of individual actors beneath dry facts, so his "Winter Telltale" (1978) reveals his knack for spinning a bawdy yarn, this one about a con man who gets himself in dutch with his ladies, that comes off as both comic and convincing. His more recent fiction in *Callaloo*, "Once a Wars' October" (1984), is more interesting still. Derrick Cunningham is a football player, like the hero of McCluskey's second novel, but playing for an Ivy League team in 1962, indeed *on* the playing field during the outbreak of the Cuban missile crisis. His young world is threaded with elements of that era—Beatles music, a young Cassius Clay, racial attitudes that now seem archaic—which, Derrick comes to realize, are painfully ephemeral and somehow precious. In other words, in "Once a Wars' October," McCluskey forces memory to speak, conjuring the drama *and* the dross of October 25, 1962, as equally important in creating the complex tissue of that moment in time. A lyrical-poetical writer, and a shrewd critic who has done valuable work on Rudolph Fisher, McCluskey reaches for new ground with every project, his most ambitious effort being an as yet unpublished novel exploring the phenomenon of black cults of the Jim Jones sort, which is, I suspect, territory untouched in Afro-American fiction.

More difficult to discuss, but no less important, is the fiction of Leon Forrest. He has published three novels: *There Is a Tree More Ancient Than Eden* (1973), which contains a preface by Ralph Ellison; *The Bloodworth Orphans* (1977); and *Two Wings to Veil My Face* (1983). All are wreckingly hard to read. This is said with great sadness, for in many ways Forrest's fiction is an archaeology of black consciousness, a fascinating search through subterranean strata of mind for mythic, folk, and psychological material fashioning the "souls of black folks." Sadly, though, Forrest does not impose for his readers a narrative pattern that would make his novels and, I'm convinced, deep insights into black life intelligible. In *There Is a Tree More Ancient Than Eden* and *Two Wings to Veil My Face,* the "story" employed to mount each novel is the simplest of event sequences: a twelve-year-old boy, for example, in the first novel, wrestling with his mother's death, and from this Forrest pulls sheaf after sheaf of cultural, historical, and mythic meaning. But without conventional dramatization. In this diagnosis I could be disastrously wrong, but fiction has often been defined, and rightly, as "dramatic narrative," where emphasis is placed, except in the most unusual of cases, on *drama,* the writer donning the hat of the playwright because certain information simply cannot be told, but must be shown so that readers can draw their own opinions, as well as on *narrative,* which, if the truth be told, is usually best used as the bridge between scenes, one the writer sweetens for readers by infusing narrative moments with the strongest voice he or she can muster.

Nevertheless, I urge readers to study Mr. Forrest's first three novels. Appreciative passages on his fiction have been written by Schultz and, most recently, by Keith E. Byerman in *Fingering the Jagged Edge: Tradition and Form in Recent Black Fiction* (1986), in which he devotes a chapter to Forrest's first two novels. Byerman tells us:

> The fictions of Leon Forrest are surrealistic in their effects. They figure forth nightmares and apocalyptic visions; they collapse and confuse the sense of time; they portray intense, often destructive emotional states; they present personal and family histories filled with coincidence, violence, and madness; and they do all this in a language that moves rapidly across biblical, street-slang, mythic, folkloric, and literary systems of discourse. He presses both language and the fictive realities it conjures up to the point of incomprehensibility. At the same time, he establishes clear boundaries.

For the vast majority of readers, these boundaries may not be clear. Byerman, however, plucks from Forrest's work his central thesis that black Americans are "orphans" who experience "abandonment, anger, guilt, namelessness, and alienation," all these conditions arising from the kidnapping of African slaves from their homeland, which pressures Forrest's characters into a search for personal identity, a theme familiar to readers of Wright and Ellison, but for Forrest, as Byerman interprets his work, "The only hope lies in accepting one's condition and drawing from the motherlike culture the strength necessary for survival." When confronted by Forrest's writing, a critic must defer to Byerman, who concludes:

> The larger meaning of Forrest's work, then, is clear: blacks have been made fatherless, motherless, and pastless by a racist society that scandalizes their being and makes them scapegoats.... This orphanhood and violence, though devastating, also makes of all blacks a community, defined by outsiders in scandalizing terms, but from within by a determination to survive through the wisdom of a folk culture....

Readers of black fiction produced in the last few years sooner or later come to realize the quasi-biographical intention of many Afro-

American authors who believe that one service they can—in fact, *must*—perform is telling stories about black people who have been written out of history. Their hope, as in the case of John Edgar Wideman's *Sent for You Yesterday* (1983), a triptych of narratives about the black residents of Homewood, is to honor their predecessors in stories that break with stereotypes and portray a piece of their lives. It is an effort to keep them alive, perhaps even to enshrine the meaning of their lives (as the author sees it) in the theater of a story, poem, or novel. Such writers have a moral obligation to remember. In Wideman's "The Return of Albert Wilkes" in *Sent for You Yesterday,* the character Carl thinks, "If I don't wake up Homewood will be gone. If I run away, far away, the Homewood streets will disappear." Much of black writing in the last decade or so is a meditation on remembrance. Praisesongs from writers who feel themselves to be keepers—or transmitters—of the past for the sake, as with Wideman, of future generations. This is fundamentally the gist of Ernest Gaines's *The Autobiography of Miss Jean Pittman* (1971) as well as of Alex Haley's *Roots* (1976); in both cases, racial melodrama serves as the vehicle for the much nobler enterprise of portraying black endurance and strength in the face of overwhelming oppression. In part, these works, when viewed together, often seem to be the *same* story recycled or sliced into from different angles, and this is troubling to the degree that one of the legacies of Cultural Nationalism (or the Black Aesthetic) is the agreement among many authors that all blacks have a shared history of oppression, which is admittedly an idea true and necessary to bring blacks together for political action, but in fiction it presents a few problems. Oversights are inevitable with such a generic, blanket view of the past. And a certain interpretative sameness is unavoidable. The question, therefore, becomes this: How have authors with a "project" such as I have sketched—if this notion is true for them—managed to achieve variety or diversity, as Reed puts it, within the framework of their common objectives?

Outstanding among these Novelists of Memory is John Edgar Wideman, a former Rhodes Scholar who published his first novel, *A Glance Away* (1967), when he was only twenty-six; followed by *Hurry Home* (1970), the story of a black lawyer's journey through European and African culture—in other words, his past—and back to a deeper involvement in the black American community; an angrier novel called *The Lynchers* (1973), which is about four black men who plan the lynching of a Philadelphia cop; yet another novel, *Hiding Place* (1981); a collection of stories, *Damballah* (1981); and, most recently, *Brothers*

and Keepers (1984), a brooding, powerful meditation on the imprisonment of his brother Rob and, on deeper levels, a grappling with the
destinies that divide brothers, forge bonds, and bring them together.
Even without further discussion, this list reveals Wideman's broad,
humanistic range of interests. In *Interviews with Black Writers,* he explains his feeling that "there is a thin line between individual and
collective experience which permits one to flow into the other," a sense
that somehow each individual reflects the Whole. Consequently, Wideman's interests in his novels, as Kermit Frazier explains in his article
"The Novels of John Wideman" (1975), span Laurence Sterne and T. S.
Eliot, as well as the black family and breakdown of life and values in
America's urban ghettos. An ambitious writer, he is also, Frazier admits,
one who "is difficult and places great demands on the reader," primarily
by a stylistic reliance on stream-of-consciousness techniques, long,
loosely constructed sentences, associative metaphors occasionally hard
to unkey, and shifting points of view. Yet this is by no means "experimental" writing in the sense of, say, Clarence Major or the Surfictionists,
for Wideman's esthetic does not break from the past. Indeed, it is
precisely the past he recovers, as an archaeologist might, in his many,
rewarding books.

Pleasures of a different sort await readers in two books, *Hue and Cry*
(1970) and *Elbow Room* (1977), by James Alan McPherson, recipient of a
Pulitzer Prize and a MacArthur "genius award," as it's called. And de-
servedly so; McPherson is one of the finest short-story writers, black or
white. He has developed an efficient and conservative prose style that
makes for one of the best, easy reads in contemporary fiction.

Unlike Delany, McPherson in *Hue and Cry* never plays with the
poetic possibilities of language and voice or with stylish sentences—
epanalepsis or anadiplosis—and the reason, I suspect, is because he's
too busy, from one line to the next, with recording as clearly and simply
as he can the lacerations and wounds of modern black life. He can be
canny and comic in "Of Cabbages and Kings," in which his narrator,
Howard, is transformed into a guilt-ridden follower of Claude, a mad
member of the Brotherhood (read: Nation of Islam), who works upon
Howard's racial guilt. But generally McPherson is our best transcriber of
pain. His title story is interspersed with dialogue passages that tell us in
no uncertain terms that simply to be alive is to be unhappy. His unnamed speaker asks, "But if that is all there is, what is left of life and why
are we alive?" And is answered, "Because we know no better way to be."

Something like a "world" emerges from McPherson's fiction. A sad one. But finally, we suspect, true. "All the Lonely People," for example, brings McPherson's considerable powers of characterization—his ability to select precisely the right details and unique quirks that bring forth a character as recognizable—to bear on the anguish of a homosexual, Alfred Bowles, whose advances throw his narrator's sense of his own sexual being into greater ambiguity. Largely, and throughout most of the stories in this collection, the grief McPherson explores focuses on our sexual and racial pretenses, as in "Hue and Cry," a tale in which black couples (and one white) continually betray each other. And themselves. Of course, this must be said with caution. For McPherson's palette is broad enough, and the point of his brush precise enough, to render suffering people on what seems the longest of continuums: the Irish janitor James Sullivan in "The Gold Coast," a lovely story about a black man's journey to committing his life to writing, and Doc Craft, the "Waiter's Waiter," in what may be McPherson's most anthologized story, "A Solo Song: For Doc."

In "A Solo Song" we have what may be one of the few portraits in black fiction of the worker as an artist of sorts, someone who, as in the case of Doc Craft, obliterates himself to give "good service" to others. Is he cut from the cloth of Ellison's Lucius Brockway in *Invisible Man?* Yes, but McPherson takes the portrait of the black worker, "the machine inside the machine," further by opening us to a moment of history among Pullman porters, a flickerflash in time that vanished—and with it a way of life—with the death or retirement of members of the "Old School" of waiters, those who didn't rely on rule books like the greenhorn waiter this story is addressed to. Leroy Johnson, looking for work, finds it and is renamed "Mister Doctor Craft" by the other blacks. Being *crafty,* we learn, is a virtue among these men, in fact a necessity because the characters in "A Solo Song," black and white, find themselves in a common, uncontrollable situation involving need and mutual exploitation, one of McPherson's favorite themes. This moment he writes about, 1916, centers, on one level, on men who ride the rails; on another it is a complex hour of American history, when massive black migration from the South to the North was undertaken, when only service jobs and menial labor were open to black workers, and when lynching and Jim Crow legislation and antiblack literature dominated race relations. What McPherson shows, brilliantly, is that regardless of those influences, Doc, Sheik Beasley, and Uncle T. Boone not only adjusted themselves in order to survive, but they also pulled from that impossibly grim situation a performance in their work that brims with grace and beauty. They created something that could not be codified in books.

But built into the situation of Doc and others is a double sort of exploitation. These men are loved because they can be exploited; they allow themselves to be exploited *so well* that the railroad owners ultimately become dependent on them, much as Hegel's slave gets the upper hand on his master by learning as a servant all the activities his master has blinked, or become rusty at doing. Ironically, the Commissary responds to this situation by developing a rule book based on spontaneous black style, a move that systematizes and, therefore, makes their performance mechanical, stealing the life and substance from what the men have created. To make matters worse, the Commissary then changes the rules whenever it pleases to force out the black waiters of the Old School, which is the form of betrayal employed to eliminate Doc Craft. Another interesting feature of this story is Uncle T. Boone's claim that the black waiter has lost his humility. When Doc Craft works, as a member of the Old School, he is apparently physically and psychologically part of the service he gives—he offers himself, obliterates himself, as only a black man of that time could do. Into this service Doc pours everything from the black experience just as, after a fashion, a blues singer takes the simplest line and overdetermines it with meaning. None of this, of course, can be captured in rules, books, or the memoranda issued by the Commissary. There is no system here; the entire service is an unrepeatable gesture, just right, because it is faintly unconscious.

McPherson knows people, black and white. Male and female. Being a smart writer, he knows politics, too. But fidelity to character, and what I would dare to call universal suffering, is always center stage in his stories. Apprentices would do well to read his books several times, if only to unlock the logic of plot in, say, a story such as "Hue and Cry," in which the action quietly, subtly assumes a dialectical pattern: Margot Payne, a brilliant black woman reeling from a failed, interracial love affair, grudgingly gives her affection (very cool at first) to a black Housing Office employee named Charles Wright, "a fellow of average intellect and even less perception," someone spurned by the younger women he's chased until they see him with Margot; as their interest in him grows, so does Charles's consciousness of how attractive he is, which leads him to several affairs, increasing betrayal of Margot, who changes—in classic anamnesis—from a woman who pitied him to one desperately in need of his love. It all works. It works very well, for McPherson, like any other great writer, understands the commingling of folly and grief found in the human heart.

Knowledge of why people behave as they do is one way to make a story convincing, the difficult process of stripping bare a life so that we, as readers can *see* how others and by implication ourselves might arrive at a certain place. A rule for this, perhaps, is knowing one's characters thoroughly, even what their telephone numbers might be (Sinclair Lewis boasted of such knowledge) and, even more to the point, knowing what things they fear most, exactly what social situations terrify them, and what has caused them the most paralyzing pain. Knowing these things, good writers, gifted with what some call "a cruel eye," then proceed to maneuver their characters into precisely those situations they dread most to face, applying maximum psychological pressure upon them, recording each of their responses as the drama unfolds, the result being either that the overwhelming stress will partially or completely destroy them before the story's end if they cannot change or that they will triumph, if they can. Of course, there are no "hard and fast" rules in creative writing; I'm only presenting a principle that works more often than it fails because it forces a writer to attend closely to moment-by-moment action achieved, as novelist Larry Woiwode says, by "painful exactitude through accumulated detail." Woiwode explains this approach to the Convincing, in "Mickelsson's Ghosts: Gardner's Memorial in Real Time" (1984), by stating that good enduring fiction is "fiction in which no sentence can be lifted from its particular paragraph without doing some violence to the rhythms or the movement of the story through time. And so it is fiction that contains a clear sense of time . . . whether to reveal dislocations in time or not, since minute-by-minute time is the most universal dimension of reality. . . ."

Woiwode reminds us that in great stories, in the dramatic element of fiction, when we feel as if we are experiencing a play, our sense of time is slowed, so that each gesture by a character, each change in pitch in a speaker's voice, each line painted on the background of a stage, and each prop is brought into relief and reinforces, as Poe might have it, the overall emotional effect the skillful writer is trying to create. Nothing is neutral, as I've tried to show in the example of Wright's *Native Son*. Minimalist writers sacrifice this kind of power in fiction, leaving us, I'm afraid, less than convinced. It isn't to be found in McPherson, who achieves the Convincing by other means. You need the novel form,

especially a good, long novel to delicately conjure thousands of concrete, specific details, then symphonically orchestrate them in a work
that feels organic, whole. In David Bradley's second novel, *The Chaneyville Incident* (1981), this species of enchantment happens often
enough to make him a writer of solid achievement.

Bradley has said, in his 1984 interview in *Callaloo,* that *The Chaneyville Incident,* winner of the 1982 PEN/Faulkner Award, is largely influenced by the writing of Robert Penn Warren, a statement that reveals
more of his tendency toward self-mockery than this fascinating book, a
historical novel about the historical imagination itself. As a story it
concerns a young and talented (though dry) black historian named John
Washington, who, against the setting of Bedford, Pennsylvania, must
unravel several mysteries: the enigma of his father, Moses Washington; a
slave catastrophe that happened a hundred years earlier; and the coming to terms with his white girlfriend, Judith, the descendant of slavers.
In these pages he brings to his readers some of the excitement and
downright mystery of historical exploration, much as a murder mystery
might, but a closer comparison—Bradley's own in the novel—is that of
the hunter or "tracker" ploughing through a dense forest of documents,
musty relics, and "cold facts" that constantly refuse to offer up their
meaning until the tracker's imagination is put into play. "History" and
"memory" are presented here as problematic, the former as a shame-
lessly hermeneutic or interpretative quasi science based—as Bradley
explains in one of his several essayist interludes—on premises inher-
ited from Herodotus, Newton, and Heisenberg; and the latter as a shape-
shifting phenomenon capable of changing before our eyes as we chase
it. For the first time in black American fiction, the racial past begins to
appear, in *The Chaneyville Incident,* as partly a product of imagination, a
plastic and malleable thing freighted with ambiguity.

It's true that Bradley is, like Wideman, a Novelist of Memory (he was
Wideman's student), but the complexity of history as a project to be
achieved, and only momentarily, raises this novel several steps above
other books of remembrance that naively see history as a *donnée.* For
the character John Washington, the effort to excavate the past, despite
the impossibility of doing so, is quixotic but necessary because "I
learned that knowing nothing can get you humiliated and knowing a
little can get you killed, but knowing all of it will bring you power." In a
sense, then, to control the interpretation of the past is to control others;
in John's methodical attempt to reconstruct the deaths of a band of

runaway slaves buried in Chaneyville, we see the need to free them, to free himself, and also to free in a backhanded way the whites who have kept the catastrophe buried and who live in fear of John's arrival. These elements are brought together at various times in the novel, though most powerfully in a scene where John, returned home to "find out where the lies are," confronts Randall Scott and his father (the Judge) during the final disposition of Moses Washington's will. Here, Bradley's eye is as cleanly focused as the lens of a camera:

> The room was large, subdued, solid, rich . . . deep. There was no way to compare it with Scott's office. . . . The air itself was different; it seemed thicker, almost as if it were dust-laden. But it was impossible to be sure, for the sunlight was blocked out by heavy drapes; the only light came from an odd ugly Edwardian floor lamp that sat in a far corner and from a simpler green-shaded lamp which sat on the desk. The desk itself was old—not antique, just an old oak desk that had been made with care and kept with love. There were nicks and scores in the wood, but years of oil and tender rubbing had healed the wounds, until now they were only fading keloid scars. Behind it sat the Judge.

No, this descriptive passage is not particularly poetic. But it is complete. Bradley "dresses the set" of the room carefully, using each prop to invoke atmosphere and to prepare us, as the camera pans the study, for the old man himself; he is not described in physical details only, since they would not tell us enough, but instead, like all Bradley's characters, in terms of a complete, biographical Sketch:

> He was a local legend, a regional projection of an American political phenomenon, the local boy who had risen by means both fair and foul to become a minor dictator, loved by some, hated by many, feared—and if the truth were to be told, needed—by all. He had been born of Scotch-Irish yeomen who had farmed land near Mount Dallas, an area noted for its independent peasant stock, but which was neatly owned and handily dominated by the Hartley family, whose history included having come over on the *Hyder Ali,* the French bottom which had brought America the final version of the peace treaty between England and the Colonies, and having quartered President Washington when he had come west to supervise the putting down of the Whiskey Rebellion. By the time the Judge was born, the Hartleys were firmly ensconced as local aristocracy, having purchased the farm at Mount Dallas from the original peasant settlers, and were doing a formidable business in freight and iron. There had been, so tales would have it, a constant friction between the Norman-English Hartleys and the Scotch-Irish peasants; not a feud exactly, but . . . at one point three of the

younger Hartley boys had been found beaten senseless in a ditch, and before the day was done the judge had left the local schoolhouse, where he seemed to be perpetually assigned to the fourth grade, and had started walking east. In two days he crossed a hundred miles of mountains and made it to the state capital. He was thirteen.

Through 432 pages, the author constructs Sketches of places and people as authoritative as this one, making *The Chaneyville Incident* a remembrance novel for an entire region of America. However, it would be misleading if I left the impression that the novel has no faults. While evocations such as this one give Bradley's novel density, they remain static; the characters so fully rendered do not change or provide much action to propel events forward. Consequently, John is forced to tell most of the story he is reconstructing about the slave tragedy to Judith, who quietly listens as long pages of essayist dialogue replace plot, especially toward the novel's end, which seems desperately hurried in order perhaps to meet a publisher's deadline; this was a contract book, Bradley explains in his *Callaloo* interview, and he fell months behind schedule.

Regardless, *The Chaneyville Incident* is one of the most intelligent black novels to come along in some time. John learns that "if you cannot imagine, you can only discover cold facts, and more cold facts; you will never know the truth," which is of a different order than data or discrete biographical items. Truth must reveal the connections between facts or present—as Bradley shows—a theory (fiction) linking all the fragments. Everything hinges on this, the *how* of shaping the silent, immense pile of contradictory facts we inherit, and on our belief that all the facts *do* somehow cohere, if only we can discern the pattern in the historical puzzle. And so, the historian's whole being must come into play; his passions inevitably fuel the hermeneutic, language-circumscribed enterprise of history.

In many ways, Bradley's ideas on history are prefigured by the distinguished German philosopher-historian Hans Jonas. In "Change and Permanence: On the Possibility of Understanding History," Jonas writes, "The understanding of history is on a par with the understanding of a work of art."[2] He adds, "We are left with *empathetic imagination* as the mysterious power operating in historical understanding. . . ." History, as our creation, a thing Western man has brought into being, thus seems a fragile thing, as Jonas explains, because the premise that change is fundamental for our being "expresses a Faustian decision rather than an ontological truth." One day, it's clear, man may not "have" what we understand to be "history." Or, put differently, the relatively recent conception of the historicity of human beings as developed over the centuries may someday vanish.

The *Chaneyville Incident*'s vision of history is simultaneously Western in its assumptions and nationalist in its thrust. Historical knowledge (interpretation) is, quite simply, a means to political power. A weapon. Thus, when Judith asks John, "Is that what being a historian means— hating for things that don't mean anything anymore?" he replies, "No, it means hating things that still mean something. And trying to understand what it is they mean, so you can hate the right things for the right reasons." For Bradley's angry, often violent young historian, "history is atrocious," a field of undisclosed crimes against black people; he supposes that "that's the basis of it all; hate, black people, white people, those simple things," and the long-hidden lies fester and spoil like the corpses of slaves in a Chaneyville cemetery. This isn't an entirely grim book, however, insofar as John and Judith clear the space for an honest, historically clarified life together after John's agonizing evacuation of the underside of Chaneyville's past. At times the book is too talky, a problem with much intellectual fiction, but it leaves a reader with a great deal to think about and cannot be forgotten.

The authors I've so far singled out present some of the most artistically and philosophically interesting writing by black males since 1970. There are, beyond all doubt, many other admirable writers who have published work in this period, and the last thing I wish to do is to slight them. I've not mentioned James Baldwin very much, as you've probably noticed, but only because he is so well known, nearly an institution now, probably the very embodiment of our consciousness of political crimes against the poor and oppressed, a courageous man who has intensified everyone's sensitivity to dilemmas involving race and sex; we could not have reached this critical juncture in black fiction without his overwhelmingly important, selfless contributions as an author and front-line fighter for civil rights. His personal life, one senses, has become thoroughly objectified, intertwined at so many points with national history that one instantly thinks of Baldwin when the subject of race arises in any conversation. He is one of America's finest, most emotionally honest essayists, and without hesitation I confess that my fledgling notions of what black fiction should be—as illustrated by my first six, clumsy novels—was shaped by Baldwin's many essays, novels, stories—that is, the "protest novel" oriented toward race politics. He is, and must always be seen as, a hero. But the "protest novel" is not my province, for esthetic reasons that should be clear by now, and so I mention him only in passing, though with profound respect.

Similarly, I've spoken little of contemporary Cultural Nationalist writers. No one should doubt, not ever, the contribution of these men and women. Or their value. The truth, which is hardly said enough, is that black writing of the 1980s stands on the shoulders of the confrontationalist fiction of the Angry School. Without it, we could not stand at all. Or have a basis to see beyond its shortcomings. Joseph R. Washington, Jr., who was chairman of the Afro-American studies department and a professor of religion at the University of Virginia in 1973, addressed these matters persuasively when he wrote:

> The theology of Black Nationalism is African communalism. The ideology is Black separatism. The philosophy is socialism or the dictatorship of the proletariat complete with the thesis (Black is right), antithesis (white is wrong), and synthesis (Black over white). Its aesthetic is cultural *elitism* based on a faith in people of African descent, a hope grounded in revolutionary people through a politics of Black consciousness.

Washington's essay, "Black Nationalism: Potentially Anti-Folk and Anti-Intellectual" (1973), acknowledges the significance of the efforts nationalist historians have made to show the diverse ways African peoples contributed to world civilizations, but he notes that "they are notoriously selective in their historical uses" and sadly contemptuous of European achievements and the many sources of black American folk culture, central among these being religion. "Neither thought nor time has been given to the depth of knowledge behind the folk faith," writes Washington. "Despite its undeveloped intellectual dimension, the folk religion has been singular in Black cultural creativity. There is more to it than has yet been plumbed." His argument is uncontestable; the richest, most enduring source of black American culture is found in the black church. And I can say, personally, that the community in which I was raised in the 1950s, one comprising black people transplanted from the South decades before, was bonded by the religious piety of my parents and the parents of my friends. Many of our social gatherings were church-sponsored. My father told his white employers he categorically could not work on Sunday, no matter what they paid him, because "Sunday was for church." He loved the rich oratory of black preachers.

The voices of his neighbors and relatives raised in song. The values of family life and hard work to help one's children and kinfolk.

Beginning first as a religion *imposed* upon slaves to keep them in line, which is why Cultural Nationalists wince whenever Christianity is mentioned, the black church became, not merely the means through which Western thought from Plotinus to Buber entered indirectly into the lived experience of black people, but a common, spiritual, social, economic, and political experience. It was the place where blacks could reinterpret Christianity and transform it into an instrument for worldly change. It became a racially tempered institution, one that raised funds to help the poor and to send black children off to college. Honesty demands we admit that the black church is the single most important, enduring social entity in Afro-American life, a phenomenon responsible for shaping progressive black thought from the abolitionists to the elegant, modern theological writings of Martin Luther King, Jr., Washington adds:

> The religion of the folk has a doctrine of sin and a doctrine of man. It knows the fallibility of all men, ideas, and institutions which cannot be overcome simply by giving them new color and skin. The openness of Black folk to the possibility of redeeming all men prevails because it is right and wise. Black religion does not need a surrogate. It needs strengthening through intellectual development.

This openness, depth, and breadth is missing in nationalist thought. Washington says it is simply "a new wine in old wine skins. As such it cannot"—and, as we now know, did not—"become vintage." The reason: because "the intellectual failing of cultural nationalism is that it has no understanding that we are all caught in one humanity and biosphere" and seeks instead "to create the illusion of a nation within a nation, a set of standards proposed as distinctive and unique for Black people," which to Washington's critical eye appears to be "the creation by sheer fiat of an ideological imperialism." Granted; yet one must say of Cultural Nationalism what is often said of Nietzsche: it is a seducer of youth. It can be exciting, flashy, a kind of political quick fix for those who are impatient with slow change and ambiguity. No matter what Washington or anyone else says, Christianity will remain the religion of the Black folk, but Cultural Nationalism will continue to intoxicate a smaller group within it, being tied to what Du Bois once called the ancient "battle of the color-line," and the dualistic style of thought that seems, sadly, to be our racial destiny. He tells us that "pride, identity, and power are its goals." Nationalism in its various forms reminds us that Pushkin and Dumas carried black genes, that Egypt had black kings, that the first people in India before the Indo-European Aryans arrived were the pre-Dravidians and Dravidians, who built Harappa and Mohenjo-Dara, and these were an African people, probably the ones pressed by the Veda-bearing Aryans onto the lowest rung of the caste system. It reminds black people systematically written out of white history that, as Jesse Jackson tells his followers, they "are somebody." And have value separate from their relatively recent involvements with whites. This is a crucial stage in the development of consciousness, one my wife and I insist our own children have, for how can they live authentically until they absorb in detail the history of slavery—*their* history, with all its despair and fatalism; they must *relive* it imaginatively, play through the horrible scenarios in their minds, discover their ruins in every black life destroyed by racism and realize, as well, that the contemporary racial world is still a Divided Landscape. However, to see *only* division is to see one-sidedly. But again, even reaching this racially polarized level of race-think, which harkens back to the generation of Marcus Garvey and the Harlem Renaissance and earlier, was a chore so difficult, so painful, we must cheer those who took those important steps.

Novelist John A. Williams is, according to Ishmael Reed, one writer who provides a "link between the generation born in the 1910s and the generation born in the 1930s." He is a fictional bridge between Richard Wright and nationalist writing today. Reed also calls Williams's masterful book *The Man Who Cried I Am* (1967) "the best novel of the 1960s." Like Baldwin and Baraka, Williams must be seen and honored as a hero to apprentice writers desperately searching for strong models of black manhood. For it is not easy to be black *and* a man *and* a writer in a culture that emasculates black men and places before its authors of color so many restrictions. In Williams's work there is strength united with intelligence, literary skill with scholarship aimed at restoring black self-esteem. And dignity. As the old saying has it, blacks often feel they have to do twice as much as whites to cover half the distance, and for the black artist this folk wisdom translates into writing more. Writing harder. And to do this one needs a model who has borne the brunt of discrimination and continued doggedly to deliver solid works of literary achievement and to discharge his manly duties. Williams, for me at least, is just such an artist.

Even after twenty years, *The Man Who Cried I Am* reads like a loaded pistol. Like the fiction of Richard Wright, who appears on these pages as Harry Ames, the "father" of modern black fiction, Williams's bare-knuckled narrative pommels you with an indictment of American racism and imperialism and the most completely detailed portrait of the social condition of the black writer in print. The pain here is like palpable flesh on his protagonist and alter ego, Max Reddick, an intelligent, sensitive black novelist caught in a nightmare of sexual, artistic, and political frustrations. This is life played out on the level of the stomach, the genitals, the skin, as expressed early in the book by Moses Boatwright, a Harvard graduate with a master's degree in philosophy, who is on death row for eating—yes, *eating*—a white man. Interviewed in jail by Max during his days as a journalist for a black paper, Boatwright is, in terms of literary history, a direct descendant of Wright's intellectual and mad prisoner in book three of *Native Son,* and of Bigger himself, and also echoes Ellison's Vet and Trueblood; he explains, "I took the heart and genitals, for isn't that what life's all about, clawing the heart and balls out of the other guy?" This *is* what *The Man Who Cried I Am* is about, the gutting of Max, a globe-trotting journalist-novelist-lover plagued by hemorrhoids and racial problems so varied, so international and ancient, a single account hardly does them justice.

Williams uses the occasion of this novel to record the complicated, often unknown history of race relations from World War II (Max served with the famous Tenth Cavalry, the Buffaloes, the 92nd Division of black Indian fighters) through the civil rights turbulence of the 1950s. After World War II Max appears on the front line of the movement for integration and continues this role into the 1960s, when the movement becomes more paranoid, more militant, and less patient with religious leaders like the character Paul Durrell, "the old and comforting image of the Negro preacher as a leader." Now, in the 1960s, militant blacks, Max sees, have greater sympathy for the position of the Nation of Islam, represented by Minister Q, whose speeches in Harlem recall those of Ellison's Ras the Exhorter. In addition to being a pop history of this twenty-year period, the novel is packed with Williams's formidable, ongoing research into precolonial African history; a political critique of imperialism; an insider's look at the often depressing mechanics of New York book publishing from a black man's viewpoint as Max is determined to "do with the novel what Charlie Parker was doing to music—tearing it up and remaking it; basing it on nasty, nasty blues and overlaying it with the deep overriding tragedy not of Dostoyevsky, but an

American who knew of consequences to come"; and numerous por
traits of interracial affairs. Max Reddick is, if nothing else, a ferociously
promiscuous man, a hater of homosexuals, who, he suggests, are ruin-
ing the world of literary art, and a fierce lover of white women found in
Paris, Amsterdam, and at New York literary tea parties.

Except for Lillian, a middle-class black teacher he hoped to marry
after the war. Pregnant with Max's child, and deeply suspicious of his
ability to earn a living as a black writer, Lillian, lacking faith in their
future, has an abortion—a botched one—that causes her death early in
the novel. Max, a penniless veteran, pounds desperately on the doors of
various editors and the Urban League for a job, any job, to support them.
He lays her death at the door of racism, believing her conservative
attitudes and her unbending, bourgeois desire for security at any cost
led to this tragedy. At the same time, Harry Ames, his Mississippi-born
father figure, and a former member of the Communist party still
hounded by the U.S. government for his outspoken denunciation of
America, is first offered, then denied, a prestigious fellowship by the
American Lyceum of Letters. This insult is so stinging to a writer of
Ames's stature that it clinches his decision to leave for Europe, which
will bring him closer to Africa, where, he believes, earth-rocking
changes in black liberation are taking place.

Meanwhile, Max bitterly endures. He secures a job, publishes his
books, and rises in the world of communications by becoming a presi-
dential speech writer for a Kennedyesque politician. He sleeps around
everywhere, stays high on morphine, grimly observes the white backlash
to black progress in the 1960s, and generally lives in the greatest of pain
from cancer. It is only later in his life, at the age of forty-nine, that he
hears again from Harry Ames, who, it is generally believed by his Yankee
friends, has lost touch with the Movement in America by moving to
Europe and marrying a white woman. This contact comes after Ames's
death in the form of a document he passes along to Max from one of his
former lovers, a transcript of the mysterious "King Alfred plan" created
by the Alliance Blanc, which one of their mutual friends, an African
named Jala Enzkwu, was killed for discovering. Ames's letter says that by
the time Max reads the document Ames, too, will have been murdered.
For the Alliance Blanc is a racial conspiracy of all the European nations,
led by America, a "final solution" based on the white man's fear of
continued African independence and black revolt in the United States.
America's first strategy, Max learns, was an old one, to recolonize blacks

in Africa, but this was rejected by the Europeans; the revised plan is full-scale internment of blacks in concentration camps in the event of escalating civil disobedience, an effort involving every police and military organization on the state and federal levels. Immediate imprisonment of all race leaders is the first item on the agenda. "King Alfred" confirms for Max his suspicions that whites, regardless of their differences, are willing to unite as Aryans against blacks if their power is seriously threatened. From Leiden Max reads the document over the telephone to Minister Q, who is grateful to receive the weapon he's always needed for educating blacks in America, but a few blocks away the minister's phone is being tapped by government agents. They will kill him. And Max Reddick, too. Shortly after making this transmission, Max is murdered.

As sketchy as this account of Williams's sprawling novel is, it makes clear that *The Man Who Cried I Am* is the ultimate tale of racial paranoia: America, indeed all the Western democracies, seen as fascist in their treatment of blacks. This story seemed more than half-convincing during a decade when revelations kept surfacing about J. Edgar Hoover's harassment of Martin Luther King, Jr., and more militant elements such as US and the Black Panthers, about the government's hope to handpick a leader for black people and its efforts to pit Cultural Nationalists against black Marxists. Technically, Williams's novel is full of writerly successes, the sort of social realism that makes him a brother to both Wright and Balzac, and character portraits of men and women of all races that deliver his large, international cast with believability. But his greatest, most unusual victory is this: *The Man Who Cried I Am,* more than any other novel in memory, captures and gives dramatic form to the half-rational, half-irrational belief of black Americans that whites are programmatically committed to suppressing all people of color, that they are "out to *get* you." Even if this desperate maintenance of power means recolonization, concentration camps, or neocolonialism. Is this fictional claim credible? Well, read the headlines about South Africa. And the Nazi "Order" based in Idaho. For most Americans the political deals struck in smoke-filled back rooms by world leaders are mysterious; for blacks, doubly so, and from the period of slavery forward, with all the horrible stories of oppression that now fill whole libraries, a *feature* of the Negro soul is the undying belief that whites mean blacks no good. Not ever. That the races, as Ellison's character puts it, are eternally at war. That slavery may one day be reinstated. This novel, more than any other, dramatically objectifies blacks' deep-seated fear of a racial holocaust, the nagging, gut-pinching terror that they can never be safe in the white world because there is a *design* behind the horrible statistics of black life—the poverty, the black-on-black crime, the drugs; that these dreadful, continuing tragedies have been masterminded by ever-devious whites (Devils to a Black Muslim); and all that is lacking is the Aryan Ur-text or blueprint ("King Alfred") to make the origin of this evil, this oppression, clear.

Into the 1970s and 1980s Williams continued to deliver powerful, well-crafted books about black soldiers (*Captain Blackman,* 1972), relationships (*Mothersill and the Foxes,* 1975), and father-son dilemmas (*Clicksong,* 1982). Only a dunderhead could doubt the service he's rendered to American letters in general and, from my view, to younger writers. "Do you ever question the way you are, why you're a writer?" Max asks Harry Ames. Who replies, "Well, you're colored and you wonder how come you're a writer because there is no tradition of colored writers. Are you related to some ancient Yoruba folklorist, to Phillis Wheatley? I think about that. Then, somehow, it doesn't matter about the tradition; what matters is now . . . I love it like this; let there be a little danger to life, otherwise life is a lie."

Harry Ames's question is rhetorical, of course. The "tradition" of black American fiction has been, and still appears to be, largely that of racial protest and recording of black pain, a somewhat existential variant on this being the books of Cyrus Colter, especially his Sartrean novel, *The Hippodrome* (1973), a horror story that begins with the protagonist sitting in a Chicago cafeteria after beheading his wife (her head is in a bag beside him), then proceeds to trace his acceptance of humiliation when two black women, discovering his secret, blackmail him into performing in a homosexual circus. Other works by Colter, who is always a gripping storyteller and superb technician, as shown in his story collection *The Beach Umbrella* (1970), which won the first Iowa School of Letters Award for Fiction, strike me as less sensationalistic and explore racial grief through quieter, more everyday incidents.

And not all books in the nationalist vein end tragically. Another significant novelist spanning the last thirty years of literary production is John Oliver Killens. An uncompromising protester of inequality, to be sure, but in his 1972 "black comedy," *The Cotillion* (subtitled, "or One Good Bull is Half the Herd"), he pulls off a sustained, complete satire of black manners and class conflicts so relentless in its attack upon white,

Western values that I must say, after revisiting this book, that he is probably more successful at social comedy, at least in this novel, than Ishmael Reed is. *The Cotillion* is presented from the omniscient viewpoint of a young, aspiring writer and Cultural Nationalist named Ben Ali Lumumba (*né* Ernest Walter Billings), a world-roaming poet born in Harlem, who tells us that "I decided to write my book in Afro-Americanese" and that "I'm the first, second and third person my own damn self. And I will intrude, protrude, obtude, or exclude my point of view any time it suits my disposition," in rejection of the white creative-writing workshops he's experienced in New York.

From its opening "foreword," where Ben Ali introduces himself, *The Cotillion* comes on as a "rapping novel," a self-proclaimed celebration of Negritude that recalls, if you think about it, Chesnutt's short story "The Wife of His Youth," in which a high-society member of the "Blue Vein Society" must accept his slave past. Killens's story concerns not Ben Ali but a young Harlem girl, Yoruba Evelyn Lovejoy. She is emotionally bullied by her West Indian mother, Daphne, into participating in a Grand Cotillion sponsored by middle-class Brooklyn blacks, "big Negroes," who despise the black poor, their own southern roots, and the servile jobs that led to their position of comfort after years of struggle, and who worship whiteness in its most cartooned form: waltzes, Chopin, all the Atonist values of Reed. What Killens sets up is a biting, close-to-the-bone conflict of racial and ethical interpretations within the black community itself. The battleground is Yoruba's mind. In one corner of this fight is Daphne; she is the racially confused product of a white planter in Barbados, whom she loves, and a black woman, whom she despises. She sees herself as a queen in exile among lesser Harlem blacks, even as a British subject during her more outrageous moments of fantasy, and from Yoruba's childhood, she's insisted her daughter act like a (white) "lady." In the other corner is Daphne's husband, Matt, a very dark, down-home, unpretentious man who adores his people, is deeply loved by Yoruba for his natural race pride and because he provides his daughter with a vision of strength arising from simple, southern wisdom. As does Lumumba, who, as it turns out, was a Harlem neighborhood boy Yoruba knew in her childhood. They fall in love, to Daphne's horror since he's a "commoner." Worse than disliking low-bred blacks and Africans, Daphne, we learn, also dislikes sex, and tells her daughter a "real lady gets no pleasure" out of lovemaking.

With these ideological pugilists in place, the ludicrous preparations for the Grand Cotillion providing the novel's middle ground, and a parody of the event its climax, Killens dramatizes the agony of assimilationist views. He creates a broadly rendered, comic black world lensed through Cultural Nationalist sensibilities. And not uncritically, because Killens condemns the "pimps" and "hustlers" who heard a speech or two by Malcolm X, then grew Afro hairstyles in order to exploit the Movement. Nevertheless, his "world" is ferociously antiwhite. So antiwhite a few readers will squirm at his identification of all things European as effeminate, empty of value, or just unhip. His intended readers are, beyond all doubt, blacks who have accepted the Black Aesthetic. It is for them that he gives a merciless beating to the in-race bigotry of Daphne and her counterparts in a social club called the "Femme Fatales." He points out the integrationist excesses of a group sociologist E. Franklin Frazier identified in his famous study as the "black bourgeoisie," a petit-bourgeois class (undertakers, inventors of hair relaxers and skin creams, black journalists) with virtually no economic clout, only a fervent desire to be accepted by other Americans, even at the expense of rejecting their race. Satire, yes. And written in upbeat slang. Killens *knows* the speech of the streets. He differs from Reed, however, by dwelling on the background of characters he doesn't much care for, such as Daphne, providing her with historical background, an ultimately complex psychological life and set of personal judgments that *do* represent, painfully, the attitudes of our black predecessors. The result is that, miraculously, we recognize and care about Daphne as we would our own mother, though not without disagreement, understand her pain as our pain and her feelings of rejection by Matt and Yoruba because she knows no other way to be and is doing, according to her lights, the best she can. This means, by the end, that Killens redeems somewhat even his fictional, black foils and mouthpieces before the novel's no holds-barred finale. As a "positive," Cultural Nationalist comedy shaped entirely by radical black views on art, *The Cotillion* is funny and fascinating, a little like cross-fertilizing Thurman's *The Blacker the Berry* with P. G. Wodehouse, whose plots often involve a dim-witted member of the upper class standing in the way of true, young love, and Amiri Baraka.

Equally devoted to burlesque is novelist-screenwriter Cecil Brown, whose first book, *The Life and Times of Mr. Jiveass Nigger* (1969), received a good deal of attention when it was published. At bottom, it's a sometimes funny sex farce about a black American named George

Washington seducing, and being seduced, in Copenhagen before he realizes he must return home to help in the struggle for racial progress. Somewhat more ambitious is Brown's *Days without Weather* (1983), a story about black exploitation in Hollywood. Brown is the author of several screenplays, among them the Richard Pryor vehicle *Which Way Is Up?* so that he knows something about Tinsel Town. At first glance, the novel seems like a good idea; we have quite a few Hollywood novels, even such famous ones as *The Day of the Locusts,* but none that explores the long history and current situation of blacks in the media. Furthermore, it is a timely subject, what with the near disappearance of blacks from the motion-picture industry in the 1980s. Brown's protagonist, Jonah Drinkwater, is an unhappy, insecure stand-up comic who hopes to find himself in Hollywood. He's brought to Los Angeles by his Uncle Gadge, a wealthy black writer who sold out long ago, speaks in a horrible black dialect with homely proverbs thrown in when in the presence of powerful white producers who flaunt their bigotry ("Gadge," says a studio mogul named Grayeye, "don't I pay you enough money to come up with a good idea to exploit your people?"), and will do anything to maintain his position as their "house nigger," his cocaine habit, and the beautiful whores he hires as his secretaries. Brown's Hollywood is presented as a huge plantation. Black entertainers in film and music and stand-up comics are its slaves. It's a business, Jonah learns, that cannot tolerate truth in any form. During the course of the novel, the black actors' union revolts against the production of "Middle Passage," a demeaning film project full of racial stereotypes. Through an all-out strike they have it replaced by the more militant, historically accurate script "Black Thunder," based on Gabriel Prosser's slave revolt. However, this new project is soon betrayed. Comic Jonah goes to bed with Clea Menchan, a producer for the show; Uncle Gadge, as the studio's Negro toady and resident Tom, edits out the historically accurate material—it's an automatic reflex for him after so many years of selling out—in the script; and by the time the production begins, "Black Thunder" has reverted to "Middle Passage" and even has one scene from "Uncle Tom's Cabin," which is the film Grayeye really wished to make. In rage, Jonah exposes them all in his last stand-up engagement, which causes a riot in the club, then leads to Jonah's becoming an overnight celebrity for the ruckus he's caused. Sudden fame, he realizes at the novel's end, is Hollywood's way of silencing him.

Unquestionably, the idea here is important. But Brown's execution fails, one sees early in the book, to develop well his material either horizontally by unpacking the full potential of the story or vertically in terms of deepening our understanding of media politics, illusion, perception, and cinema. A novel such as this should do more than dish up Hollywood's use of stereotypes or dwell, as it does, on how many L.A. entertainers are freebasing. One might, for example, explore through film the power of images to shape consciousness in this, the age of teflon presidents and MTV-styled motion pictures where fast-edited visuals replace character development and even logical continuity. Instead, Brown goes for easy, predictable Hollywood clichés: promiscuous women, alcoholic producers, grumpy screenwriters who hate themselves for being hacks. And, as in his first book, he marks narrative time with leering, adolescent sex scenes that never rise above the level of pornography. Like *The Cotillion,* this novel might be called a "black comedy" that empties both barrels at the black bourgeoisie, represented here by such sellouts as Uncle Gadge, and even Jonah himself, who has at last found out who he is: "a very *angry* and *sick* and *disturbed* person, but . . . *honest.*"

Well, maybe.

While you might argue with the honesty of Brown's portrayal of movie people, the person Jonah has discovered himself to be is, in many ways, the same person we find in Williams's Max Reddick, Major's Allen Morris, Bradley's John Washington, and many other black protagonists in the fictional world of recent Afro-American writing. That is, people deformed by their lack of power in a racially Divided Landscape. Many hate themselves and whites, fear homosexuals, are drawn powerfully to women for release yet fail to sustain healthy relationships, feel a deep revulsion for the black middle class and its values, and accept, or at least give lip service to, the politics of black power, but sometimes in a halfhearted way, tilting toward Negritude but knowing its shortcomings. There are few success stories here, unless by success we mean small victories of rebellion against white, bourgeois society and the status quo. As Clayton Riley suggested at the 1978 Howard University Black Writers Conference, what has generally been explored, in books under discussion here, is "the fractured world of American racism and psychic disorder," providing, one sees, variations on the visions of Wright, Ellison, and earlier black authors; and sometimes advancing black writing technically and thematically—as in the works of Major, Reed, Delany, Young, and Bradley—but leaving the "tradition" of Afro-American letters as a literature of tragedy unchanged.

5

■ *The Women*

■ During the last decade, black writing has moved forward on two clear fronts, the commercial and in respect to content, by which I mean this: a wider audience has opened for a few black writers, and the seldom-discussed experience of black women has, like the experience of women in general, been thematized in literature, thereby bringing to light new or very old levels of social discrimination the nation needs to deal with. Like racism, the depths of sexism run deeper than most men dream, sedimenting even our scientific perceptions. For example, in her defense of the recent "New Wave" science-fiction writers, Joanna Russ, a writer as prolific as she is brilliant, points out in her 1975 interview in *Science-Fiction Studies* that some critics regard the work of Samuel Delany, Ursula Le Guin, and herself as drawing primarily from the "soft" sciences of ethnology, sociology, and psychology rather than the "hard" sciences (physics, mathematics, chemistry) preferred by writers of an earlier generation. But this very division, she points out, between "hard" and "soft" conceals a hidden sexist subtext insofar as in this culture "hard" is the metaphor for the male organ, and "soft," for the female one, the upshot being that derogatory gender distinctions are built into our scholarly judgments and phraseology. How often have we heard a colleague described as "intellectually soft," the inference being that he lacks the rigid, hard, dry character of the male member and is, therefore, womanly and weak, yielding and moist?

Going even further, Russ suggests in one of her best essays, "What Can a Heroine Do? Or Why Can't Women Write?" (1972), that even our conception of "plot" is male-oriented, if by plot we mean a series of events that emphasize external action and "rising conflict leading to a resolution," because in a male-dominated society, women have been prohibited from engaging in anything other than activities such as housework, support roles for men, and daydreaming. Consequently, she suggests the lyrical, "shapeless" form of novels by Virginia Woolf or Djuna Barnes, or non-Western forms with less rigid internal structure, such as nineteenth-century Russian novels, as being more appropriate to carry the less action-oriented experiences of women who wonder, and rightly, what their characters can *do* to keep the objective events of a story moving forward.

Phenomenologically, the questions raised by feminists strike as deeply at the presuppositions of culture and esthetics as the radical critiques of Black Nationalists and Surfictionists of an earlier era. Although the literary struggle of the sexes must be as old as the plays of Aristophanes, the modern emergence of a "woman's perspective" can only be regarded as a revolutionary, objective step forward in culture and consciousness, one that sensitizes us to the relativity of truth. We can never again innocently read fiction or watch films that slight black or female characters without wincing, never again stupidly approve images of blacks as servile or women as mere support objects for men. Regarding these negative images, our way of seeing has been changed irreversibly, and a sensitive reader must acknowledge that the fiction of, say, Gayl Jones and Ntozake Shange, is *demanded* by the suppression of black women in American literature and life, if only to make our dialogue on Being more democratic.

But it is clear that the double burden of being black *and* female adds another layer of complexity to these questions, an explosive charge, one might say. Jacqueline Jones points out in her study of black women from slavery to the 1950s, *Labor of Love, Labor of Sorrow* (1985), that the single most important entity in black life since the Civil War has been the family. Ninety percent of all female slaves in the 1850s, according to Jones, labored more than 261 days per year, for eleven to thirteen hours each day. The threat of rape was ever-present. Their offspring went neglected in a system where landowners believed that "the raising of children must not interfere with the raising of cotton." Jones argues that after Emancipation blacks opted for sharecropping over working in "gangs" as they had as slaves, because sharecropping allowed the fusion of kin and work relations into a single unit for economic and social survival. Also, it left black women free briefly during the day to be mothers, which their men fully supported. "The interests of the family," she says, "superseded individual desires," and it is this single law of black life that, on the whole, kept the race solvent through the brutal 1890s, two world wars, and the depression.

In short, blacks had nothing *but* the family to turn to for emotional and material support for most of the century. However, the facts of family life in the 1980s point to the disintegration of this fundamental, hinge-pin element for black survival. If government statistics can be believed, half the black children born today in America are born to single parents, and half of these are teenagers bound only for the most menial of jobs. The FBI reports that black males between the ages of sixteen and twenty-five have one chance in twenty-eight of being murdered, mostly by other blacks, given the rise in gang activity in the cities. The FBI has also released figures stating that a woman is severely beaten by a man every eighteen seconds in America. Military doctors report that of every 1,000 black recruits tested in 1985–86 for venereal disease, 3.9 tested positive for AIDS. According to the Census Bureau, blacks in 1984 made up 12 percent of the population—28.2 million people—earned 56 percent of the income of whites, accounted for 35 percent of separated Americans, 13 percent of the divorced, and 7 percent of those married. Black females headed 27 percent of households run by women. By 1984, black unemployment had reached 15.9 percent. Added to these startling figures is what Hortense Candy, president of Delta Sigma Theta Sorority, calls the dearth of marriageable black men between the ages twenty and thirty-five. There are only, she claims, 59 single employed black men for every 100 black women between the ages of twenty-five and thirty-four, with the ratio being even lower in the twenty- to twenty-four-year-old category. A controversial, much debated 1985 Yale-Harvard study concluded that white, college-educated women unmarried at age thirty had a 20 percent chance of ever marrying; if they were single at thirty-five, only 5 percent could expect to marry; and if they were single at forty, the odds for marrying slipped to 1.3 percent. The researchers decided that for black women the odds were even worse.

It is against this depressing, perhaps even disastrous background of the black family's internal contradictions and near collapse that we must understand the angrier work of some black women authors. They are addressing a crisis in the black social world. We must also keep in mind the obvious fact that black males have traditionally found it easier to move forward in society, even to marry whites; we've seen how often black male writers such as Wright, Ellison, Williams, McPherson, and Bradley (but not McCluskey or Reed) place their protagonists in interracial sexual situations and portray black women as bourgeois or too conservative; and we must place these works beside novelist Toni Morrison's faintly existential claim in her article "What the Black Woman Thinks about Women's Lib" (1971) that the black woman "had nothing to fall back on: not maleness, not whiteness, not ladyhood, not anything. And out of the profound desolation of her reality she may very well have invented herself."

Morrison's statement is more rhetorical than realistic, for no being except the God of the ancients comes into existence *ex nihilo,* and, whether one wants to admit it or not, all social progress today stands on the shoulders of our progressive predecessors, black and white, male and female. Rather, the important point here is that women writers of all colors have brought forth a new universal, or way of seeing. A revelation of meaning (being) that sharpens our perception of the social world. Given the seriousness of their subject, it would be, I believe, a grave disservice to these writers and to ourselves if we employ a sexual or racial double standard in evaluating their artistic and intellectual successes and failures. I'm speaking of the well-meaning tendency of some critics to use one esthetic or philosophical criterion for evaluating white male authors, usually a tough-minded one, and another, less demanding, for artists nonwhite or female since we are all of us eager to encourage creators who have been forced to overcome an ensemble of racial and cultural obstacles put in their way. But if black women's writing rests on a sound foundation, as I believe some of it does, if it does in fact reveal a common situation affecting us all, then the genuine value of the novels and stories we shall address here should be unquestionable, and two sets of criteria, unnecessary.

I've urged this mindfulness of artistic integrity when discussing black women's writing of the 1980s because, like any politically charged, oppositional fiction, it forks up deep passions that at times make clear-headed dialogue almost impossible. And also because the arguments revolving around the work of Gayl Jones, Toni Morrison, and Alice Walker have created something of a controversy bordering on crisis in the black literary community. None of this furor was caused overnight. Rather, it is the culmination of literary pressures building for at least forty years, dating back to the work of Zora Neal Hurston and Nella Larson, and earlier to the very genesis of the women's movement. However, the anthology *The Black Woman* (1970) signaled, along with other post–civil rights era works, a shift in the character of fiction by black women. It emerges as a literature distinct yet not wholly separate from the earlier Black Arts Movement of the 1960s. And much of its momentum in this new incarnation came from works by Ntozake Shange, Gayl Jones, and Paule Marshall.

Shange's choreopoem, *For Colored Girls Who Have Considered Suicide When the Rainbow Is Enuf,* strikes me as one of the first fusions of the Black Arts and women's movements. It was first presented at the Bachanal, a women's bar near Berkeley, California, in an atmosphere humming with women's consciousness-raising groups. There, "in as much space as a small studio on the Lower East Side," Shange and four friends danced, free-formed poems, and created music for some twenty patrons in December 1974. They moved their show from San Francisco to New York in 1975, fine tuning and trimming theatrical fat as they progressed. Woody King produced *Colored Girls* as a workshop under Equity's Showcase Code, and assistance came from Joe Papp and Oz Scott, who directed the choreopoem at the Henry Street Settlement's New Federal Theatre, the New York Shakespeare Festival Public Theatre, and at the Booth Theater on Broadway in 1976.

Though a collage of dance, poetry, and prose narrative, Shange's show presented the lives of seven unnamed black women for whom "bein alive & bein a woman & bein colored is a metaphysical dilemma." Note Shange's use of Baraka's spelling and stylistic flourishes. It is an experience of spiritual outrage insofar as her "colored girls"—the daughters of Senghor's deeply spiritual African Personality—suffer rape, love's rejection, the denial of their beauty by whites, and an ugly round of betrayals by black men who unfailingly violate their trust and vulnerability and then, head tipped, apologize, "o baby, ya know i was high, i'm sorry."

They are scarred and scared, these seven women, and many are the prototypes for protagonists in later black fiction. *Colored Girls* comes across as a courageous laying on of hands to heal, women healing women, because their "stuff is the anonymous ripped off treasure of the year." They want, it seems, a moratorium on their relations with men until each woman is recognized as a being of beauty and grace. Humor balances pain in this show. There can be, for example, the lady-in-brown's delightful story of Toussaint L'Ouverture side by side with lyricism, and the lady-in-red's hair-raising story of Crystal, a woman dedicated to her children, and of her man, Beau Willie, who kills them. Outrage and irony are commingled in *Colored Girls* because Shange manages to move beyond despair to the possibility of self-renewal through love, sisterhood, and the rejction of the separation of "soul and gender." For these reasons, *Colored Girls* not only fits easily into the tradition of black theater engineered by Baraka and Ed Bullins but also transcends the imperialism of male gender that dominated many earlier plays in the history of black drama.

This play is certainly more influential and important than Shange's two novels, which are workwoman-like but ordinary in subject and execution. For more interesting work in the novel form, we must turn to the fiction of Gayl Jones, whose work includes *Correigidora* (1975), a haunting "blues novel" about Ursa Correigidora, a man-battered blues singer oppressed equally by black men and generations of white males, and *Eva's Man* (1976), an even more startling novel—a horror story, Jones calls it—about a mentally deranged woman who creates a bizarre murder.

Jones, a student of the poet Michael Harper, possesses not only a good ear for spoken language but also the power to spin dreamlike, erotic narratives that show the darker side of black sexuality. In interviews, she confesses a love of Chaucer's gift for voice, the ability to don various masks for narrative ventriloquy, a talent she has herself. Her prose, though simple, has the power, the intimacy found in fiction writers conscious of the "oral" tradition of storytelling, and a confessional quality as well, as if someone were whispering into our ears. "The police came," opens *Eva's Man,*

> and found arsenic in the glass, but I was gone by then. The landlady in the hotel found him. She went in bringing him the Sunday paper, and wanting the bill paid. They said she screamed and screamed and woke up the whole house. It's got a bad name now, especially that room. They tell me a lot of people like to go and look at it, and see where the crime happened.

Jerry Ward, in his article "Escape from Trublem: The Fiction of Gayl Jones" (1982), writes, "Her novels and short fictions invite readers to explore the interiors of caged personalities, men and women driven to extremes," people who are at the edge of madness caused by sexual and racial defilement. Further examples of this can be found in her short fiction, especially in "Goosens," in which a young woman off to college visits a memorable character named Miss Goosens, a child actor in 1930s films debasing blacks. During the course of the story Miss Goosens sees herself in a television rerun of one of her old movies and identifies, horribly, not with herself at a younger age but with a white girl in the picture. She thinks, in other words, that *she* was that white child. As an artist, Jones delivers chills like this again and again, as if a trapdoor had opened suddenly, plunging us into the darkness—the webby dungeon—of another mind. And no other author has confronted the psychological brutality of black sexual oppression as subtlely and clearly as she has.

No less influential is the work of Paule Marshall, the author of four books of fiction. Her art is distinctive for several reasons, not the least of which is her dual American and West Indian background, which provides her work with an interesting interface of cultural variations within the black diaspora. And her career, stretching thirty years from her first story, "The Valley Between" (1954), to her novel *Praisesong for the Widow* (1983), is notable for both her steady production of first-rate writing and a spiritual balance and emotional maturity rare in much black fiction. Dorothy L. Denniston shows, in her article "Early Short Fiction of Paule Marshall" (1983), that Marshall's apprentice work exhibits sensitivity to the inequity in sex roles long before the issue became widespread. In the story "Reena" (1962), originally published in *Harper's* magazine, she portrays, as Denniston points out, the agony of black women like Reena who are socially punished simply for being dark in complexion: "My mother," her protagonist writes, "stopped speaking to any number of people because they said I would have been pretty if I hadn't been so dark. Like nearly every little black girl, I had my share of dreams of waking up to find myself with long, blonde curls, blue eyes, and skin like milk." Like the heroine of Zora Neal Hurston's classic, Reena is exposed to several kinds of men, white and black, who disappoint her much as McPherson's Margot Payne meets disillusioning men in "Hue and Cry," but Marshall manages, generally, through careful delineation of character, and with a far gentler touch than Gayl Jones, to present all her fictional actors in a spirt of fairness.

There are strong similarities between Killen's *The Cotillion* and Marshall's first novel, *Brown Girl, Brownstones* (1959), which is propelled by the conflict of a black mother and father with their daughter torn between them. In her article "Paltry Things: Immigrants and Marginal Men in Paule Marshall's Short Fiction" (1983), critic Marilyn Waniek writes, "The mother has accepted the crass values of the upwardly-mobile Barbadian immigrant community in which the family lives, while the father retains a dreamer's futile pride in the cruel face of American racism and disappointment. Their daughter, Selina, vacillates between these two extremes, neither a Barbadian nor an American, but a permanent and unhappy outsider. The novel ends with her escape to Barbados." A similar dramatic structure underpins part of my own novel *Faith and the Good Thing* (1974), as the heroine Faith Cross is constantly pulled between the differing outlooks of her father, Todd, and her mother, Lavidia, as well as between materialistic science and magical modes of thought; but as fruitful as this situation has been in recent black fiction, Paule Marshall is the writer who got there first. She has given us a story collection, *Soul Clap Hands and Sing* (1959), consisting of stories that expand on her interest in black people with a dual heritage and the dilemmas this causes them; *The Chosen Place, The Timeless People* (1969), a novel that extends these meditations; and *Praisesong for the Widow* (1983), her third novel, tracing the transformation of a middle-class, middle-age widow named Avey Johnson into a woman healed of her identity crisis and fully at peace with her non-Western roots. In all these works Marshall impresses one with her honest effort to explore that oldest of themes in black literature—the loss of identity—as well as the beauty of the non-American black voices she records. "Perhaps the proper measure of a writer's skill," she wrote in 1983 in an autobiographical essay for the *New York Times Book Review,* "is the skill in rendering everyday speech." This is indeed one measure, though not the most important, more of a natural gift than a thing easily teachable, and is one of the many splendors in Marshall's important, steadily improving body of work.

However, the greatest praise for technical prose mastery among black women must go to the much-celebrated Toni Morrison. More than any other contemporary writer, she is a direct descendant in style and sensibility of Ralph Ellison. Perhaps even his rightful heir in her ability to place fictional excellence above political appeal, yet without softening the social importance of her works. I cannot say that she is formally innovative. She has not thematized form in the fashion of Major or Reed. Or offered the kind of intellectual vigor and insight found in Bradley. But as with Toomer, one of her formidable talents is for shaping a precise, spell-inducing prose that creates both musical and mythic elements in her novels, certainly in *Sula* (1973), a beautiful, race-transcending exploration of evil and existential freedom presented through the lives of two women in a small town in Ohio. Observe this remarkable novel's opening:

> In that place, where they tore the nightshade and blackberry patches from their roots to make room for the Medallion City Golf Course, there was a neighborhood.

The initial, kick-off phrase "In that place" brings the time-suspending incantatory sort of opening found in fairy tales. Already, the reader is transported from the realm of naturalism to a black universe where the fabulous—magical realism—may occur. And indeed does in Morrison's fiction. She sustains this nearly hypnotic voice and tone through the musical possibilities of alliteration, which takes the form of hard consonants (*t*hat, *t*hey, *t*ore, nigh*t*shade, roo*t*s) and the more rolling *r* sound (to*r*e, blackbe*rr*y, *r*oots, neighbo*r*hood), creating an aural tension in the line, a counterpoint of sounds, and finally ends with the authoritative voice so typical of the tale, "there was a neighborhood." One can endlessly dwell on this kind of careful, precise use of poetic language and symbolic skill in Morrison's prose, but she provides larger delights, too. She writes persuasively at times from the viewpoints of men as well as of women, as demonstrated in her hugely successful novel *Song of Solomon* (1977), a bestseller and winner of the National Book Critics Circle Award. This is, as I read it, a mystery novel, highly textured with details of black culture, about Macon (Milkman) Dead, Jr.'s effort to achieve self-knowledge and to recover his past. A past that reveals, a reader is startled to discover, a confirmation of the black myth that Africans could fly. Or at least Morrison uses it as a metaphor for liberation from the death the Dead family has endured for so long. In more than one sense, Morrison fits the mold of Frye's writer with an "educated" imagination, first because her approach to exploring racism is through the manipulation of cultural archetypes (folklore), and second in that, as a teacher and former editor at Random House, she is familiar with paradigms and devices in black fiction's history and bends them toward fabulous variations or toward the concerns and viewpoints of black women.

But, like critic Arthur P. Davis, I'm inclined to believe that Morrison's first two novels, *The Bluest Eye* (1970) and *Sula,* are stronger, tighter novels than her two later, more complex works, including *Tar Baby* (1981). On the negative side, one must say of Morrison, as Davis does, that "she too often 'tells' us what the characters think and do [and] does not 'render' her material," relying more on her gifts for narrative and brilliant metaphoric uses of speech than on dramatically structured scenes. True, *Song of Solomon*'s symbolic pattern, as Chiara Spallino suggests in her article "*Song of Solomon:* An Adventure in Structure" (1985), is a tissue of racially interpreted folklore that intrigues. But, artistically, the abstract symbols are not made to live through action, or by the fusing of idea and event. Consequently, the novel's pacing is off, and her tendency to pad out sections of *Song of Solomon* leads to a loss of propulsion or *oomph* in the novel until the end.

And, as in many other black novels, Morrison's fictional universe seems lacking in light and balance. Now and again, unsympathetic portraits of whites and also of black men surface. These elements are troublesome, but despite such faults, Morrison emerges as one of the truly outstanding and influential black writers of the age, the sort of writer intelligent critics of both races can respect for both her hard work and her personal courage. She is, one must remember, single-handedly responsible for the promotion of such younger black writers as Gayl Jones, and in both her person and her performance she has helped create bridges of dialogue between the races and the sexes.

Many black writers, it seems, have difficulty grasping the rhythm and logic of dramatic scene and plot, the fluid, natural flow of unmediated action. If Morrison's talent lies primarily in the direction of mytho-poetic narrative, her capacity to ensorcel more through "telling" than "showing," the reason can be found in the fact that many Afro-American authors lack extensive training in the principles of drama but naturally find themselves surrounded from birth by a treasure of unique black voices or original ways of speech based on southern folk idioms, West Indian parlance, the rich oratory of the church, inner-city slang, and even for a few the tribal languages of the Academy. Don't get me wrong. Most contemporary fiction by white authors in our time also lacks a masterful sense of dramatic scene, that special moment in fiction when the opposing aims of characters force them into a collision that changes them before our eyes, leading them toward self-discovery or a moment of recognition (the classic formula is desire A is opposed by obstacle B which produces new emotion C) that becomes in the best literary art the very core or heart of a novel, a story, or a play. Even so diversified a talent as Toni Cade Bambara falters in her first novel, *The Salt Eaters* (1980), when called upon to achieve "presentedness" through drama. Her charms as a truly comic writer, however—a relentlessly funny "rapper"—are second to none.

Bambara is not so skilled at descriptive elegance as Morrison, nor does she match Morrison's gorgeous imagery, but she is wonderfully funny. And comedy is *hard*. Timing is everything. And so is good taste. To fail at being funny, as any stand-up comic can testify, is to fail abysmally. To "die" on stage. Which Bambara never does. Her strength is snappy, hip dialogue and an ever-crackling narrative style that absorbs all forms of specialized dictions. When need be, she is colloquial. Yet also scientific, folksy, or spiritual. Whatever's necessary to make her sentences boil and bubble over with a distinctive black woman's brand of humor and exuberance. Who else would tell us that black women know when their men have been "sleeping white" because their rhythm is off? Manic, sometimes even frenzied, Bambara's style sends sparks flying off the surface of any subject she attacks. And "attacks" *is* the right word, for in *The Salt Eaters,* the story of bottomed-out Movement people hungering for the experience of "wholeness" after their civil rights efforts collapse, Bambara uses her original blend of satire and grief to batter at social hypocrisy, then offers us a measure of hope. Consider how her character Velma Henry sees a male race leader:

> Exhausted, she was squinting through the dust and grit of her lashes when the limousines pulled up, eye-stinging shiny, black, sleek. And the door opened and the cool blue of the air-conditioned interior billowed out into the yellow and rust-red of evening. Her throat was splintered wood. Then the shiny black boots stepping onto the parched grass, the knife-creased pants straightening taut, the jacket hanging straight, the blinding white shirt, the sky-blue tie. And the roar went up and the marshals gripped wrists and hoarsely, barely heard, pleaded with the crowd to move back and make way for the speaker. Flanked by the coal-black men in shiny sunglasses and silk-and-steel ties, he made toward the platform. . . . Some leader. He looked a bit like King, had a delivery similar to Malcolm's, dressed like Stokley, had glasses like Rap, but she'd never heard him say anything useful or offensive. But what a voice. And what a good press agent. And the people bought him. What a disaster.

From narrative such as this she shifts easily to dialogue that isn't exactly a transcript of spoken speech—no, not that, but stylized, scintillant, and satisfying:

> "You know as well as I, Old Wife, that we have not have been scuffing in this waste-howling wilderness for the right to be stupid. All this waste. Everybody all up in each other's face with a whole lotta who struck John—you ain't correct, you ain't cute, and he ain't right and they ain't scientific and yo mama don't wear no drawers and get off my suedes, and he hit me and she quit me, and this one's dirty, and that one don't have a degree, and on and on."
>
> "Min?"
>
> "Don't they know we on the rise? That our time is now? Here we are in the last quarter and how we gonna pull it all together and claim the new age

in our name? How we gonna rescue this planet from them radioactive mutants? No wonder Noah tried to bar them from the Ark. Hmph."

Despite Bambara's highly energetic prose, *The Salt Eaters* tends to sprawl shapelessly, occasionally losing focus and a clear through-line of development, which suggests that she is still working to make a smooth transition to the novel from the short story, the form in which she has distinguished herself since the 1960s. Admirers of her shorter works, myself included, often point to her story "The Lesson," from her collection, *Gorilla, My Love* (1972), as indicative of her skill. Here, in a first-person voice spun from the clever brogue of street kids, she writes of the visit of poor black children to a toy store for the rich, a place so offensive in its illustration of the inequity of wealth in America that one of her characters can say, "Imagine for a minute what kind of society it is in which some people can spend on a toy what it would cost to feed a family of six or seven," and Bambara's protagonist, as well as the reader, is changed forever.

But it is *The Color Purple* (1982), beyond all doubt, that stands at the crest of black women's fiction in the 1980s. Alice Walker's punchy, third novel is the publishing phenomenon of this decade. It is probably the most commercially successful novel in the entire history of Afro-American letters and has spawned a few imitators as well as electrified the black writing community, especially after its reincarnation as a major motion picture by a director as influential as Steven Spielberg. Its fans and detractors are legion, among them black lesbian feminists who have seldom seen Negro homosexuality portrayed with humanity and compassion. More generally, it numbers among its supporters readers who see in Walker's book elements presented but never so widely celebrated in fiction by other black women, these including the explicit sexuality found in works by Gayl Jones, the sass and style perhaps of Shange and Bambara, and the longing for reconnection with one's African roots, which is, of course, a theme as old as Cultural Nationalism itself. Added to this, Walker adopts a refreshing literary form or revitalizes it in her use of an epistolary format to structure her story; this is probably a first for Afro-American literature, though in 1986 Nathaniel Mackey used the same form for his reflections on black music and culture in *Bedouin Hornbook*. And she provides ruminations on the nature of God that open into the five-millennia-old vision of the deity as a being without attributes. In Hindu philosophies such as Advaita Vedanta this notion is central, but not until *The Color Purple* has such a theologically interesting thesis been presented in the field of Afro-American thought, unless it be in my own *Oxherding Tale* (1982). And fairness demands that we credit Toomer with having raised this idea first. No matter how one might object to the Hype that elevated this novel into a massive bestseller, or wonder, as many do, whether it actually is Pulitzer Prize material, or wonder over the dubious judgment of the Academy Award officials in denying its film version any awards whatsoever, a reader simply must acknowledge that Walker's book is a very good, though perhaps not great, technical performance that is the literary expression of an immediate social revolution of the highest importance. Just as Harriet Beecher Stowe's *Uncle Tom's Cabin,* which is by no means a masterpiece, became the rallying point for abolitionist efforts a century ago. And, finally, one must confess that *The Color Purple* is not even, as I now write these words, a *book* any longer. It is a cultural event.

Cultural events, I hope you'll agree, are hard to judge by merely literary standards. Judith V. Branzburg observes in her 1984 *Callaloo* review of one of Gloria Naylor's books, "For Afro-American women writers the perils of politics and art are more numerous than for men. Not only must the women remain true to their race, they must also support racial unity by not being too hard on black men." And in his lengthy article, Mel Watkins notes:

> For those black women writers who have chosen black men as a target have set themselves outside a tradition that is nearly as old as black American literature itself. They have, in effect, put themselves at odds with what seems to be an unspoken but almost universally accepted covenant among black writers ... of [not] exposing aspects of inner-community life that might reinforce damaging racial stereotypes already proffered by racist antagonists.

Walker's bestseller is impaled on the horns of this dilemma, which we shall return to in a moment, a quandary applicable only to politically motivated fiction. We can agree that the general evidence for a few sociological shortcomings or oversights in *The Color Purple* is pretty much in by now. The men portrayed in the novel, from Celie's step-father to Mister and Harpo, are, on even casual inspection, thinly rendered strawmen created essentially to be foils for the unfailingly wise, heroic women—Celie, Nettie, and Shug Avery—to overcome in their bid for selfhood, spirituality, and black sisterhood. There's little reason to repeat these criticisms in full, because other writerly problems exist in *The Color Purple*, the foremost of these being the novel's overall sketchy treatment of the complexity of race and social relations in post–World War I Georgia; put another way, it lacks the "spirit of place" required by the Sketch. Similarly thin are its characters, and plot is also a problem inasmuch as the story feels imposed upon the people depicted, especially the men, who are made to say and to do things that perfectly fit the author's polemical design but that cannot count, in traditional dramatic terms, as revelation of character. Furthermore, it has been argued that even the lesbian love affair between Celie and Shug Avery is more a matter of telling than of showing, so that the deeper logic of single-gender attractions, the power of this coupling, is not so compelling as, say, the more deliberate, delicately sculptured fiction of James Baldwin. In fact, a good deal of *The Color Purple*'s drama is propositional, happens off-stage, is disclosed through dialogue or through Celie's missive to God as opposed to unfolding before our eyes, the exception being the startlingly effective scene where Celie tells off Mister. Shug Avery's theological-ontological statement on the qualityless character of God is a case in point. The artistic question here is, how does one concretize such an intangible assertion? Walker doesn't, thereby leading one to conclude that, despite the novel's confrontational punch, it is not fully realized as a work of art.

Walker's earlier novels, *The Third Life of Grange Copeland* (1970) and *Meridian* (1975), are stronger artistic achievements than her third, and Arthur P. Davis praises both highly, yet admits in his essay "Novels of the New Black Renaissance" that *The Third Life of Grange Copeland* reveals a degree of awkwardness and that "too much of the work [is] *told* rather than rendered." For all this, what Walker tells is of importance. While her men may be one-dimensional, their behavior—like that of Reed's voodoo dolls—presents through social caricature the darkness of black male attitudes toward black women. When one of her characters reports that sex with a man is on a par to being used as a toilet, the male reader cringes, this being the sort of subterranean fear many men do in fact have. If we are honest with ourselves, we cannot deny the tincture of exploitation that resides in some cases of heterosexual relations. This is not an idea new with Walker. One need only reread sections of Sartre's *Being and Nothingness,* and, I would suggest, all of Simone de Beauvoir's *The Second Sex,* to find the same.

Added to the novel's stature as one of the most important protest works since Wright's *Native Son* and Baldwin's *Another Country* is the obvious fact that Walker is polymathic, producing works of short fiction (*In Love and Trouble,* 1973), poetry (*Revolutionary petunias,* 1973), and essays of cultural exploitation that extend through analysis her fictional arguments. By herself she has spearheaded renewed interest in the career of Zora Neal Hurston, her efforts in this direction creating for Hurston a critical and popular appreciation delayed by nearly half a century of neglect. And she has lately become a publisher. In 1984, her Wild Trees Press released *A Piece of Mind,* a story collection by J. California Cooper, who, Walker says, writes in the folk vein of Langston Hughes and Hurston. All these elements make the clumsier moments in *The Color Purple* forgivable, reminding us that this book is part of an ever-growing *oeuvre* that, in the Sartrean sense, is a "project" of singular importance.

Yet it would be wrong to leave the question raised by Walker's book before returning to the curious points made by Branzberg and Watkins. Should black authors practice self-censorship, hiding the blistering sores and uglier scars of Afro-American life from whites in order to present a unified, racial front? Walker, one must admit, does candy over the worse shortcomings of her female protagonists, thereby maintaining, as a feminist at least, a solidarity of sisterhood. So that, after two thousand years, it appears we are still ensnared by the problems of truth and poetry as first defined by Plato's *Republic.* I mean this need by a particular group, whether it be dominant or powerless, to strictly control the images we present to the world, Ellison's sense that individual utterance may endanger the group. We should call this by its proper name: lying. And worst of all, lying for political advantage. Self-censorship, for whatever reason, violates the truth-seeking *telos* of literature, which requires a complete disclosure, all the facts and let the chips fall where they may, *saying* in order to *show* more clearly a situation so that it can be responded to with courage. If literature and philosophy have any integrity, or any teeth whatsoever, it is in the pursuit of truth at all cost, even into the pit of hell. Even if it demands an artist stand utterly alone. Even if the price is a prison sentence, social expulsion, or death, as it is in totalitarian societies. Any political group that plays fast and loose with the truth to attain its goal, or any author, spoils the very foundations on which that goal, regardless of its nobility, rests. *The Color Purple* demonstrates, if nothing else, this: the priority of freedom. Our obligation, as artists, to reveal and to name crimes. And yes, triumphs, too. To be *open,* as Alfred North Whitehead once phrased it, to "the adventure of ideas."

Also of importance among black women who have managed to meld the concerns of feminism and the Black Arts Movement in their writing is Gloria Naylor. Her book, *The Women of Brewster Street* (1982), which received the American Book Award, consists of seven beautifully written, powerful interlocking stories about tragedy-burdened women. In many ways, this is a remarkable performance. Like Toomer's *Cane,* especially like his sketches of women in the first section, it straddles two genres, those of the novel and the short story. And it may also be compared to Sherwood Anderson's *Winesburg, Ohio* in the way Naylor evokes Brewster Place and its people with a superb eye for detail, a convincing grounding of their lives together in a location as fully rendered as Bradley's Chaneyville.

In her first story, "Mattie Michael," her protagonist is abused by three men: Butch, a southern boy who impregnates her; her father, a seemingly religious man, who beats her horribly when he learns of her pregnancy; and her baby himself, Basil, whom she coddles and over-protects so thoroughly that he never grows up. Naylor flirts dangerously here with Daniel Moynihan's thesis of black woman as a castrator of males; Basil kills a man accidentally and, after Mattie puts up her house for bail for his release, he skips out on her and the authorities. This embittered woman becomes the matriarch for all the others in Brewster Place. They include Etta Mae (all the stories except for the last are named after the women characters), who feels that "all the good men are either dead or waiting to be born," a sentiment Hortense Candy would probably agree with. Regardless, she goes after a dazzling preacher in a nearby church. As it turns out, he's a lecher. Etta Mae simply wants to snare him to improve her material condition in the world, but fails, resigning herself to manlessness after Reverend Moreland T. Woods takes her to a hotel, then dumps her. A more pleasing character is Kiswana Browne, who, in the wonderfully wise story devoted to her, comes to terms with her middle-class mother. Kiswana (*née* Melanie) is a cashiered 1960s black militant living now in poverty on Brewster Street, the daughter of proud, well-to-do Negroes long involved in the NAACP and civil rights. As Naylor traces the argument between the two women, Kiswana comes to see the heroism in her mother's quieter, steadier approach to social reform and even learns that her boyfriend and her father are both into women's feet as sexual objects.

More tragic is the story of Luciela Louise Turner, who feels that her daughter, Serena, is the "only thing I have ever loved without pain." She loses this child when her baby shoves a metal object into an electrical socket at nearly the same moment Ciel's no-good, insensitive, abusive husband, Eugene, for whom Ciel has secretly aborted their second baby to stop his cursing her for saddling him with babies and bills, is packing, preparing to leave, lying baldly about having a job that will take him away to another city. Ciel loses everything. She goes into a physical and spiritual decline until Mattie rocks her; then, in a scene much like Marshall's redemption of Avey Johnson in *Praisesong,* the older woman washes the younger one in a ritual of cleansing and renewal. From this kind of tragedy, Naylor shifts again to lighter work in "Cora Lee," an enchanting tale about a welfare mother indifferent to her children. Cora watches the most abysmal soap operas, surrounded by her bedraggled brood of children from several different men as they destroy systematically the apartment around her. Kiswana Browne brings one of Cora's boys home after finding him eating from the garbage cans behind their building. She sees the sort of ruin Cora lives in; then, with twice the patience of Saint Francis, since Cora is trying to ease her out the door so that she can return to her soaps, Kiswana gets her to agree to take her children to a black, open-air production of *A Midsummer Night's Dream.* Cora complies, begrudgingly scrubbing her kids clean. At the performance something magical occurs: her kids, who she thought would shame her, are enthralled. And Cora is too, remembering her own love of Shakespeare from her high school days before she got pregnant, when she was, in fact, a good student. In the actors on stage she sees her own lost possibilities but also the chance that one of her children might someday be up there, bringing pleasure to others through art. By the story's end, Cora has changed, found a light she'd lost, and the reader is forced to conclude that Naylor has wizardly powers as a writer.

Naylor's story "The Two," however, stokes up other feelings. It is about two lesbians on Brewster Street, Lorraine and Theresa, the former the "passive" member of this couple, who longs to be liked and loved by everyone else, the latter the rougher, more "dominant" personality. They become the subject of gossip, and even hostility, when a boarder named Sophie attacks Lorraine at a tenant's meeting arranged by Kiswana. Lorraine flees the meeting but can't return to Theresa, with whom she's had a lover's spat, and is befriended by the old janitor, Ben, a wino whose life is full of lacerations—white racism in the South and a nagging wife who left him. Together, in his basement rooms, they talk and console one another. Their comradeship is splendidly presented, but Naylor moves her heroine to disaster: four black punks, worshippers of Shaft and Superfly, torment, then jump Lorraine one evening, maiming her as badly as the sacrificial woman "Tralala" in Hubert Selby's *Last Exit to Brooklyn*. She is nearly mad after this experience, torn apart inside, lying in the alley when a drunken Ben stumbles upon her. Lorraine, not knowing what she is doing, or who he is (or does she?), smashes at his head with a brick, over and over, jellying the old man's brains.

As anyone with two eyes can see, these are gut-wrenching, powerful stories. No denying, of course, that some use racial and sexual melodrama to move the action forward; and, except for the old sot Ben, nearly every black male in this book resembles the Negro Beast stereotype described so many years ago by white racists as the brutal, stupid creature of violent sexual appetites. But I'm willing to go on record as saying that Gloria Naylor is a profoundly talented writer. Her experiential "world," its parameters and possibilities, is identical to those of Shange (indeed, this book reads like a novel version of *Colored Girls*), Jones, and Walker, but she *knows* her women more deeply than the others, and is able to place this knowledge of people on the page with greater authority. And that in fiction is all that counts.

For purposes of comparison, I urge readers to look at Kristin Hunter's *The Soul Brothers and Sister Lou* (1969). Although not so technically accomplished as Naylor's book, Hunter's novel follows the adventure of a teenage girl who is intelligent, light-skinned (a "Red," or redbone), and lonely in her ghetto neighborhood. Hers is the typical "welfare family" of the 1960s   the father is gone, absenting himself so as not to be in the way after he's unable to find work; her brother, William, a postman with dreams of being a printer, takes over the father's role and respectfully yet painfully listens as his mother, who, like Marshall's matriarch in *Brown Girl, Brownstones,* tells him not to strive for too much in a white man's world. Sister Lou convinces him to rent an abandoned storefront church to set up his printing press and to let a gang of boys she wants to impress use part of the space for a clubhouse. What Hunter tries to achieve here is a story about members of a ghetto community pulling together against tremendous odds, each member changing for the better as they learn the value of cooperative effort. William learns that he's no different, really, from the street hoodlums, one of whom is a Black Nationalist named Fess, an ultimately tragic boy, brighter than all the rest, who bullies Lou about being a Tom, she learns, simply because light-skinned girls have rejected him all his life.

The problem with Hunter's novel, which surfaces halfway through the book, is that in order to provide tension she needs an antagonist, a villain to keep the action rolling. This she finds in a monster named Officer Lafferty, who enjoys beating up the teenagers in her neighborhood. He raids the clubhouse when he hears gang members are having a party to raise money for one of their projects. During the raid a boy is killed, Sister Lou's cheery optimism turns sour, and the book lumbers from one 1960s social cliché to another. Hunter's intent, however, is stronger than her skill: namely, to show that even some whites—teachers at her school—are for these kids trying to pull themselves up by their own bootstraps and provide such assistance as they can. It's a flawed, weakly conceived story that seems dated almost twenty years later. But it reveals much about the effort by some black writers to achieve balance and fairness in their portraits even during the heyday of the Black Arts Movement and just before feminism became generally available as a dominant shaping social ideology in the thought of Afro-American authors.

Even more successful in this regard is a strangely wonderful novel called *Let the Lion Eat Straw* (1979) by Ellease Southerland. Southerland's language and syntax are, one first thinks, as simple as those in a child's primer; they disarm the reader by disguising to a degree the way her style creates exactly the right overall rhythm for tracing the entire life of her heroine, Abebe Lavoisier. In the years between the two world wars, she is transplanted as a child from the South to Brooklyn to live with her mother, Angela, and her stepfather, Arthur, a black man whom Southerland portrays as the embodiment of kindness, someone Abebe (her name means "African flower") learns to adore. But Arthur dies, leaving Abebe and Angela in a worse economic bind than before. Abebe meets her real father, Robert Lee Watkins, an irresponsible and unpleasant man, and her Uncle C-J, who molests her some fifty times during her teens. However, Abebe has learned from Arthur how kind some men can be; she manages to excel as a pianist, as her stepfather had wanted, and by the age of nineteen is playing for her church, where she meets a young, visiting preacher named Rev. Daniel Torch from St. Augustine, Florida. Abebe marries Daniel, but waits until she is pregnant to reveal how Uncle C-J abused her, a fact that violently unsettles Daniel. His is a mind easily unsettled, we learn (and Abebe learns too late), and his mental instability dates back to his childhood. This fact is disclosed when Daniel forces Abebe to return with him to his family's home in Florida for the birth of their child. There, he slips into a deeper madness, is hospitalized, and Abebe and his relatives stay by his side. Once he recovers, they return to Brooklyn, now with several children, open a bakery during World War II, and prosper. Abebe writes plays that become the center of community celebrations; survives an episode when Daniel's brother, Calvin, is wrongly accused of raping and murdering a white woman (this very pious, prayerful family sees Calvin through this injustice); sees her husband endure more bouts of near mental breakdown before he goes onto medication permanently; and, at last, lives to witness their move to a three-story house on Long Island and the growth of her children. She has fifteen before her womb is removed.

Readers will see soon enough in *Let the Lion Eat Straw* that Southerland covers incidents treated by other black writers and sets up situations that seem as if they will lead to grief. But her goal lies somewhere else: her people endure. They are almost perfect figures for Joseph R. Washington's idea of "the folk," who through loving and leaning on one another during times of hardship create lives of strength and self-fulfillment. What does Abebe think of Daniel? His illness troubles her during their life together, but when thinking of him, her words are "My husband. My best friend." Even as all of us know despicable characters like Walker's Mister and Naylor's Reverend Moreland T. Woods, we know Southerland's people, too. They are our older, black neighbors. And relatives. Their lives quietly blend heartaches and unheralded victories. Many of them, like Southerland's Abebe, leave life's stage with a feeling that the long journey, so full of setbacks, has been worthwhile, even made beautiful when they see their children grown and their parents placed in easier material circumstances, and when they look at their spouses from across the great distance of three dozen years of shared history, love, and dreams.

Although Southerland takes on the difficult chore of describing an entire life, many writers, particularly those Novelists of Memory I've mentioned, place their characters in the world of childhood. Creative-writing teachers and editors can report of reading with unsung heroism thousands of stories about protagonists who are children "coming of age." We are made to watch them discover sex. Or having their first menstrual flow (but it takes an imaginative writer such as Susan Thornton to use menstruation metaphorically, tying it into dramatic scene and theme, as she does in her short story "Jason" [1983]). Or trying to unlock the mysterious, hypocritical behavior of adults. Good novels and stories in this vein usually succeed when the *issue* the child faces is one that still has an immediate meaning for adult readers. But most of these stories fail. Young writers select a child-protagonist often because they, being in their early twenties or late teens, find the problems of childhood nearer at hand and easier to express than those gummier, more ambiguous ones of adults. I'm not saying the problems of childhood lack complexity; they don't. But apprentice writers with little to say sometimes conclude, wrongly, that they can avoid a subtle treatment of Big Issues or adult themes by inserting the reader into a prepubescent viewpoint.

Sad to say, this happens in *Annie John* (1985), written by the talented short-story author, Jamaica Kincaid, whose work frequently appears in *The New Yorker*. While we can argue that Naylor's book satisfies the novel form in an unconventional way, *Annie John* must be judged, not as a novel, but as an attempt to link a collection of eight, first-person short fictions. In these, young Annie recalls growing up on the island of Antigua. There isn't much in the book to write or to think about, for these pieces have only the most minimal sense of Forster's "story." Basically, the book comes down to this: Annie is an intelligent girl who sees herself as wicked, though Kincaid never convinces the reader of this. Had she been truly wicked the book might have moved toward interesting possibilities. As it is, Annie simply muses about the meaning of death, tells us about her love for her girlfriend, Gwen, describes her first menstrual period, and generally vacillates between loving and hating her mother, who is faultless. This is not a book in which much happens, not even sharply focused reflection. Nor is the island of Antigua delivered to the reader through historical and cultural Sketches that would have provided setting and grounded the characters. Generally, I stump endlessly for the importance of "universality" in black fiction, but I'm afraid that here the universality of Annie's growing up translates into vagueness, emptiness, and far too few specifics (as Aristotle notes, the universal is embodied in particulars), the result of all this being that one leaves the world of *Annie John* as untouched, as unmoved, and as clean as when one entered.

Much the same can be said of the science-fiction stories of Octavia E.

Butler. Nevertheless, her fiction is unusual and worthy of attention, even when her novels lose their focus or plunge so deeply into fantasy that revelation of everyday life, which fantasy at its best is, disappears. Butler's novel *Wild Seed* (1980) begins promisingly enough, being first set in Africa, then in an American settlement. It develops the strange relationship between two Africans, a 4,000-year-old, body-stealing mutant named Doro, who collects sensitives and other people of unusual abilities from all over the world in order to take over their bodies and to breed people like himself, and a centuries-old oracle named Anyanwu. Anyanwu is a "wild seed," the last of a bloodline almost extinct. Doro, sensing her power, selects her to provide magical children for him and physical bodies he can inhabit at will since Doro has no body of his own. Early in the novel Doro is presented as monstrous, a Nubian enslaver of other Africans, one whom even European slavers fear in the seventeenth-century landscape of the book's opening scenes. Powerful servants obedient to him are scattered over the globe. As an immortal, he is ruthless, lacks all feeling, thereby suggesting satanic, truly frightening designs in his callous manipulation of others. We wonder: What is this odd creature up to? What plans does he have for Anyanwu? Is he the Devil? Are events in real history traceable to the hitherto unknown manipulations of an African god cursed never to die? But Butler chooses not to develop her story along the culturally fascinating lines embodied in her opening. Instead, she focuses, perhaps too narrowly, on Anyanwu's ineffective battles with Doro, over control first of her own body, then of those of her children, one of whom, named Nweke, Doro sleeps with in total indifference to Anyanwu's tribal horror of incest, and this leads to the child's death. Feminist concerns crackle just below the surface action here. Ultimately, Anyanwu flees from Doro after taking a century of abuse and, being a shape-shifter herself, hides from him by assuming different bodies, then establishes her own secret community of magically empowered people, which she protects.

The same unusual theme of a black who breeds monsters reappears in Butler's *Clay's Ark* (1984), a book indebted in its basic idea to Michael Crichton's *The Andromeda Strain*. As usual, Butler's prose is effective, though timid, taking no risks with language, yet creating a clear narrative and crisp dialogue. Also, her insertion here of what seem to be medical facts about viruses is fun. Set in a future world where some cities have degenerated into nightmarish sewers and where "car gangs" without homes live a nomadic life, this is the story of a black astronaut, Elias Doyle, the only survivor of a psychically powered spaceship called

Clay's Ark, which returns from a trip to the second planet of Proxima Centauri with a deadly organism that gives its victims enhanced sensory powers and an uncontrollable desire to infect as many people as possible. Eli, we learn, infects a family of white farmers and sets up a breeding colony on their land. Naturally, he must bring in new members to infect. The sickness in him demands new hosts. And, as the novel opens, he kidnaps a doctor, Blake Maslin, and his two mulatto children, Keira and Rane, though race here is not significant for the children or Eli. We might simply call this affirmative-action casting. The book details their fight to escape from Eli. All three are infected with the extraterrestrial life form and become animal-like in their senses and hungers. The two girls live in fear of what sort of children they might produce after seeing one of Eli's offspring, a beautiful, swift, beastlike boy of five who moves about on all fours. To shorten the story, Dr. Maslin and his kids conveniently escape after overcoming their powerful captors, but they are captured by a murderous car gang, a fate worse than being at the mercy of Eli's mutating family. The gang members rape Rane, then behead her; Dr. Maslin dies during the assault Eli's people launch on the car gang to get the Maslins back, and Keira returns to the community of mutants as the novel ends on a grimly prophetic note: American cities are being torched by citizens in an effort to control the spreading intergalactic affliction that will, the reader concludes, consume the entire planet, producing a strange new form of mankind, as in the remake of the film *Invasion of the Body Snatchers.*

In this recent novel, Butler creates tension by two familiar devices. First, she alternates chapters between the past and the present, between describing in the odd-numbered sections Eli's fight to survive after he crash lands back on earth and, in the even-numbered sections, Dr. Maslin's efforts to save his doomed children from Eli. So far so good. But the second device, so overworked in the history of pulp fiction, proves less satisfactory. What keeps us reading, in this second case, is the fact that Butler withholds crucial information (who are these people capturing Maslin, why are they doing this?) as a means to force us to move forward. Similarly, in *Wild Seed,* we are introduced to Doro sniffing out Anyanwu's whereabouts in Africa, then mysteriously whisking her away onto one of his slave ships, our interest being simply that of finding out the specifics of what sort of creature he is. Butler puts off telling us any of this, or laying her cards on the table, in each of the two novels until the last possible moment, usually halfway through the book. Genre fiction, especially mysteries and detective tales, often rely on such duplicity. But once we've been told, we readers tend to sigh "Oh," and the novels have nowhere to go on the level of original storytelling and invention. We read on, drubbing our fingertips on the table impatiently, to get the basic information of character and situation that a less commercially minded author would have provided earlier. And always we ask, "How does this illuminate life and feeling in the contemporary world?" Butler withholds the very premises of the story as a strategy for building suspense, as if she doesn't quite trust the integrity of her people and their problems to carry the forward momentum of the story to places that will surprise. Butler's scenes, therefore, consist of dialogue and exposition rather than dramatic exploration of character and plot. Her decision as these two books unfold is to retread continually material cryptically introduced in earlier chapters until we uncover, wearily, what we should have been told after only twenty or thirty pages of reading. Hers is not yet a great contribution to science fiction. But her imagination seems endlessly fertile, capable of putting us in the remote past or the hypothetical future. Once her powers "to suppose" are united with complexity of character and her fantasy creations are controlled by stories aimed at stripping bare our lives as we live them, Butler may well deliver a crucial addition to the field of speculative fiction in general and feminist science fiction in particular.

To conclude this chapter, it might be helpful to recall Morrison's statement on the black woman's quest for identity. Analysis of the novels under review shows this search, far from being finished, has only just begun. It is more at the stage of criticism of social crimes than of presenting a coherent, consistent, complete "identity" for black women, one that distinguishes its essential elements from Cultural Nationalism or Negritude. Historian Jacqueline Jones quotes Michele Wallace's 1982 observation that "despite a sizable number of Black feminists who have contributed much to the leadership of the women's movement, there is still no Black women's movement, and it appears there won't be for some time to come." The conjoining of race and sex, we see, thematizes the black experience in hitherto unexplored ways, but it *triples* the number of philosophical and political dilemmas to be resolved in the pursuit of selfhood. Du Bois might have said of black women writers of the 1980s that they ever feel their "threeness; an American, a Negro, a woman; three souls, three thoughts, three warring ideals in one dark body."

We should also return to a point made by Joanna Russ in her essay "What Can a Heroine Do? Or Why Can't Women Write?" Well, obviously, they *can*. And in the cases of Morrison, Naylor, and Marshall, with gorgeous prose. But, as Russ tells us, the Lifeworlds of the women characters we have looked at differ significantly from those of black male writers in many important ways. They are generally about sexual and domestic relationships. For the most part, they are worlds centered on the home, child raising, the church, service on political organizations, and quieter—less violently action-oriented—events than, say, the worlds of Ellison, Wright, and Williams, unless the action takes the form of rape or beatings or other events that women as a group fear. The result, and our reward as readers, is that these women have, by and large, a sharper eye for the small nuances and tics and eccentricities of human behavior than their male counterparts do. They key in on character psychology more quickly. And nearly all of them are prose singers, golden-throated speakers with a musician's ear for the possibilities of beautiful utterance. The Pulitzer Prize–winning poet Rita Dove, for example, when she turns from poetry to short stories in *Fifth Sunday* (1986), masterfully transfers her skill with language to creating short sketches brimming over with character observation and a tight, controlled line. And how are many of them on plot? Not quite so polished or powerful. And on formal virtuosity? Here again, this esthetic dimension seems to be of little interest to black women writers, the exception being Walker's third novel.

Joanna Russ has written variations on the heroic fantasy, sword-and-sorcery tradition created by such authors as Robert E. Howard, inserting her warrior-heroine Alyx in suspenseful "adventures" simply as a way of claiming this exclusively male, externally directed, world-manipulating sort of story for women; the technique is, for phenomenology, that of "free imaginative variation," as philosopher Don Ihde discusses it, and minority authors have often employed it for fictional ends: that is, by inverting or altering the larger literary tradition for their own goals. Recall Reed's inversion of detective and western stories. With black women authors, this taking over of popular forms has not been the case, and the reasons, as Russ explains in her essay, are obvious: until recently, women were denied social roles that led to such fiction. The implication is that as social options increase for black women, their fictional worlds will expand, developing a repertoire of subjects, themes, forms, and genres as seemingly boundless as their gifts for poetry and song.

■ *Afterword*

■ Over twenty years ago, in his critical study of black fiction called *Black on White* (1966), David Littlejohn caused a stir in some circles when, after discussing Afro-American novels published before 1966, he concluded:

> A white reader is saddened, then burdened, then numbed by the deadly sameness, the bleak wooden round of ugly emotions and ugly situations: the same small frustrated dreams, the same issues and charges and formulas and events repeated over and over, in book after book. Economic repression, dehumanization, ignominious role playing, the constant dealings with the very bottom of the human heap—the responding spirit is dulled, finally, bored by the iteration of hopelessness, the sordid limitation of the soul in the tight closet of the black imagination.

Many writers and critics simply dismissed Littlejohn's judgment as biased or, at best, insensitive; but his conclusion is disturbing enough, and painfully true enough, to deserve further exploration, particularly when we realize how perfectly it echoes an earlier evaluation by black critic Blyden Jackson in his essay "The Negro's Image of the Universe as Reflected in His Fiction," which was reprinted in *Black Voices* in 1960. Jackson wrote, "It seems to me that few, if any, literary universes are as impoverished as the universe of black fiction. [Of greatest interest] are the things that cannot be found there." Jackson and Littlejohn were responding to what I call the overwhelming technical and thematic one-dimensionality of much black fiction published prior to 1970, the apparent lack of adventure and creative ambition in Afro-American letters, the tendency by authors of color to plow the same racial and social ground over and over when an entire universe of phenomena lay waiting for investigation. One question for this study, obviously, must be to ask whether in two decades this situation has significantly changed.

As noted earlier, Cultural Nationalism and the Black Aesthetic have, despite their numerous shortcomings as systematic thought, shaped much black American fiction, and it's not by accident that the once broad hearing given this ideology coincided with the rise of other forms of cultural critique in the period of the 1960s. I am referring to an entire generation's renewed interest in humanistic Marxism, feminism, various styles of Eastern metaphysics, and the entire collection of "countercultural" thought in the air by 1968. Cultural Nationalism shares with these other assaults on bourgeois life an apparently new American hunger for spirituality, moral values, breadth of vision, and a retreat from materialism in its more vulgar forms. At least in its intent, Cultural Nationalism hoped to move black fiction beyond "dealings with the very bottom of the human heap." The political ground from which it springs is a sickened reaction against racism, individualism seen as selfishness and opportunism, American imperialist adventures after World War II, corruption in government and business, and the denial of black racial identity uncritically accepted by a few early proponents of integration. As such, the primary thrust of Cultural Nationalism is the reaffirmation of the hope of black men and women—many of them from the baby-boom generation, with its conditioning to expect ever-improving quality in life—that they can lead lives of deeper creativity and spirituality. And this priority is evident in some of the Black Aesthetic's more interesting adherents, younger poets such as Peter Harris, editor of *Genetic Dancers,* a California magazine devoted to positive images of black fatherhood, and author of a lovely collection of children's stories called *Wherever Dreams Live* (1982), in which even bricks and trees cooperate with his characters to build a universe that is livable and just. But most of Cultural Nationalism's followers have failed to create a convincing, enduring art because, as Nathan Huggins wrote in *The Harlem Renaissance* (1971) of their predecessors in the 1920s, "The dilemma is a tough one: the race consciousness that is so necessary for identity most likely leads to a provincialism which forever limits possibility of achieving good art. . . ."

No, the Black Aesthetic produced preciously little "good art," and even less capable of lasting. The various styles of black feminism have, I believe, fared better in the fiction of Naylor and Marshall. But, like Cultural Nationalism, it sometimes teeters on the brink of sexual provincialism, lacking the balance required by fiction that transcends polemics or political agendas. Regardless, the deeper levels of oppression discovered by black women writers have breathed a bit of renewed interest into black fiction. This has not resulted in a new "renaissance." We're still only talking about five or six well-known black women authors, but they have provided a new wrinkle on American protest fiction, one backgrounded by Cultural Nationalism's demand for social morality and propelled, generally, by the present wide interest in feminism.

Sadly, then, some of the "deadly sameness" of sensibility and sight Littlejohn spoke of still overshadows the bulk of black writing, the outstanding exceptions being Bradley's foray into the philosophy of black history, Morrison's mythic narratives, Major's explorations into European forms of experimentation, Walker's efforts at formal invention, McPherson's nearly brutal emotional honesty, Reed's seriocomic satires, and Young's gentle, balanced worlds of humor and spirituality. These authors strike me as more venturesome than most within a tradition that, as one bookseller friend recently remarked to me, has nearly become a branch of "genre fiction," dominated, like Harlequin Romances and pulp westerns, by strict social formulas and calcified ways of seeing. Credit for changing the grim judgments of Littlejohn and Jackson must, however, also be given to the more original and entertaining writers not so theoretically systematic as those I've mentioned, but whose works push our imagination, our sense of the possible beyond the everyday—Walter Dean Myers, for example, the author of *The Young Landlords* (1979) and several other highly popular books for young adults. Next, and no less important, is Samuel Delany and such other newcomers to speculative fiction as Octavia Butler and Steven Barnes, author of two episodes for "The Twilight Zone" television series and four novels, including *Street Lethal* (1983), *The Kundalini Equation* (1986), and *Dream Park* (1981), and two novels co-written with Larry Niven. Even more unusual, Barnes is also a contributing editor to *Black Belt* magazine, America's oldest martial-arts periodical, where his column on Eastern fighting philosophy appears regularly. More than most other writers, these authors confirm Reed's statement that black fiction, far from locking us into a single, limited approach to art and life, can be sufficiently diverse to carry us toward new experiences and "ways of being eminently more human," as Clayton Riley says. We can also expect good work in the future from MacArthur Fellow Jay Wright, who over two decades has demonstrated his ability for depth and complexity in intricately woven poetry and plays. And also from former philosophy student and musician Percival Everett, who has produced two novels,

Suder (1983) and *Walk Me to the Distance* (1985), which, although flawed, demonstrate an ever-growing individuality and impressive control of fictional technique for a novelist barely thirty years old.

Criticism can rightly conclude that black writing has evolved in terms of the subjects and styles it takes as its own, and this slow change is, as one might expect in any literary period, largely the conscious, steady work of a handful of serious writers, what you might call Du Bois's latter-day "Talented Tenth" drawn from a total of roughly two hundred novelists and poets at work, according to Poets and Writers, by the mid-1970s. Does this small fraction of pathfinders seem depressing? God forbid. Rather, the fact that black fiction philosophically still remains a form of genre writing—which is one of the reasons so many apprentice black novelists who rushed into print during the dizzying 1960s now find trouble marketing their manuscripts, find, in effect, the *Zeitgeist* of the 1980s less inclined to publish a writer simply because he is black—this fact, I am saying, tells us in no uncertain terms that a new seriousness and skill will be required from black fiction writers of the future. And that the numerous "things that cannot be found" in black writing, as Blyden Jackson phrases it, should not be seen as an unfair condemnation of Afro-American authors, but as the most thrilling of challenges. This idea suits me down to the ground, the possibility that our art can be dangerous and wickedly diverse, enslaved to no single idea of Being, capable if necessary of unraveling, like Penelope, all that was spun the night before and creating from entirely new social and scientific premises if need be, or adjusting the seminal work of the past to address issues relevant to this age.

For in the domain of literature, as in the field of philosophy, there can be innumerable starts, an endless series of new excavations of experience, but nothing that even remotely resembles a conclusion. I am reminded of Edmund Husserl's remarkably sad yet revealing lament in a letter written in 1904 to his teacher Franz Brentano: "I am now forty-five years old and I am still a miserable beginner." This, after a lifetime of writing and rewriting that led to a revolution in philosophy. It could well be the motto for any fiction writer, for with each story we are obliged to return to wrestling with and rethinking the most fundamental aspects of literary arts. Each new story teaches us what a story can *be,* which underscores for a serious artist the necessity of approaching racial and social phenomena in a humble, patient spirit of listening and letting be whatever the world wishes to say to us.

"Everyone," Schopenhauer wrote in *The World as Will and Repre-sentation*, "must stand before a picture as before a prince, waiting to see whether it will speak and what it will say to him; and, as with the prince, so he himself must not address it, for then he would hear only himself." And so it is for both the critic and the creator of fiction. Such egoless listening is the precondition for the species of black American fiction I see taking form on the horizon of contemporary practice, a fiction of increasing artistic and intellectual generosity, one that enables us as a people—as a culture—to move from narrow complaint to broad cele-bration. When we have finally crossed this great distance, the prehistory of Afro-American literature will end. We will not have "black" writers or books long out of print and collecting dust in Black Studies libraries, or even sporadic fads that briefly inflate the bookstores with fictions as ephemeral as soap bubbles. Rather, we will see a fiction by Americans who happen to be black, feel at ease both in their ethnicity and in their Yankeeness, and find it the most natural thing, as Merleau-Ponty was fond of saying, to go about "singing the world."

Notes for Philosophical Works

1. Being and Race

1. André Malraux, *The Voices of Silence,* trans. Stuart Gilbert (New York: Doubleday, 1953), p. 281.

2. *The Collected Dialogues of Plato,* ed. Edith Hamilton and Huntington Cairns (Princeton: Princeton University Press, 1961), p. 284.

3. John M. Anderson, "The Source of Tragedy," in *An Invitation to Phenomenology,* ed. James Edie (Chicago: Quadrangle, 1965).

4. Martin Heidegger, *Being and Time,* trans. John Macquarrie and Edward Robinson (New York: Harper and Row, 1963), p. 179. I refer the interested reader to the entirety of section 30 in chapter five, where "fear" as a phenomenon-disclosing intention is discussed.

5. Karsten Harries, *The Meaning of Modern Art* (Evanston: Northwestern University Press, 1968), p. 158.

6. William Earle, *Public Sorrows and Private Pleasures* (Bloomington: Indiana University Press, 1976), p. 66. In his first section, "Ideology," Earle provides an extensive, eloquent, and, one might add, hilarious critique of philosophical errors in the rhetoric of the 1960s.

2. Being and Fiction

1. E. M. Forster, *Aspects of the Novel* (New York: Harcourt, Brace and World, 1954), p. 86.

2. Maurice Merleau-Ponty, *Sense and Non-Sense,* trans. Hubert L. Dreyfus and Patricia A. Dreyfus (Evanston: Northwestern University Press, 1964), p. 26. Of particular interest here is Merleau-Ponty's essay "Metaphysics and the Novel," as well as his principal work, *The Phenomenology of Perception,* trans. Colin Smith (London: Routledge and Kegan Paul, 1962).

3. Don Ihde, *Existential Technics* (Albany: SUNY Press, 1983), p. 97.

4. William Gass, *The World within the Word* (Boston: Nonpareil Books, 1979), p. 314.

5. William Gass, *Fiction and the Figures of Life* (New York: Random House, 1972), p. 17.

6. Mikel Dufrenne, *The Phenomenology of Aesthetic Experience,* trans. Ed-

ward S. Casey, Albert A. Anderson, Willis Domingo, and Leon Jacobsen (Evanston: Northwestern University Press, 1973). Of critical importance is Dufrenne's chapter "The Truth of the Aesthetic Object," in which he argues that reality does not need to be represented for it is already present; art is, instead, a revelation of truth that transfigures the real or the so-called objective facts.

7. Maurice Merleau-Ponty, *The Prose of the World,* ed. Claude Lefort, trans. John O'Neill (Evanston: Northwestern University Press, 1973), p. 133.

8. Jean-Paul Sartre, *Saint Genet* (New York: New American Library, 1971), p. 285. And one is also drawn to Sartre's statement, "Language is a *nature* when I discover it within myself and outside of myself with its resistances and laws which escape me: words have affinities and customs which I must *observe,* must *learn* . . . and words sometimes display surprising independence, marrying in defiance of all laws and thus producing puns and oracles within language; thus the word is *miraculous*" (p. 276).

9. Alfred Schutz and Thomas Luckmann, *The Structures of the Life-World,* trans. Richard M. Zaner and H. Tristram Englehardt, Jr. (Evanston: Northwestern University Press, 1973).

10. Herbert Spiegelberg, "Phenomenology through Vicarious Experience," in *Phenomenology: Pure and Applied,* ed. Edwin W. Strauss (Pittsburgh: Duquesne University Press, 1964).

11. Guy Murchie, *The Seven Mysteries of Life* (Boston: Houghton Mifflin, 1978), p. 357.

12. Maurice Merleau-Ponty, *Adventures of the Dialectic,* trans. Joseph Bien (Evanston: Northwestern University Press, 1973), pp. 138–39.

3. Being and Form

1. John Gardner and Lennis Dunlap, *The Forms of Fiction* (New York: Random House, 1962).

2. Northrop Frye, *The Educated Imagination* (Bloomington: Indiana University Press, 1964), p. 40.

4. The Men

1. Raymond Federman, *Surfiction: Fiction Now and Tomorrow* (Chicago: Swallow Press, 1975), p. 14.

2. Hans Jonas, "Change and Permanence: On the Possibility of Understanding History," in *Explorations in Phenomenology,* ed. David Carr and Edward S. Casey (The Hague: Martinus Nijhoff, 1973), p. 118.

Index of Authors and Titles

EDITOR: *Karen S. Craig*
BOOK AND JACKET DESIGNER: *Matthew Williamson*
PRODUCTION COORDINATOR: *Harriet Curry*
TYPEFACE: *ITC Garamond Light with Helvetica Black*
PRINTER AND BINDER: *Haddon Craftsmen, Inc.*

CHARLES JOHNSON is director of the Creative Writing Program at the University of Washington, a Guggenheim fellow, an NEA fellowship recipient, a former board member of the Associated Writing Programs, and Fiction Editor of *The Seattle Review*. He has received the Writers Guild Award (1986) for his PBS drama "Booker," the Callaloo Creative Writing Award (1983), the Washington State Governor's Award for Literature (1983), and Southern Illinois University's Journalism Alumnus of the Year Award (1981), and has published numerous short stories, critical articles, drawings, book reviews, and written for many television series.